My
Turn On
The Swing

by David B

Published by WriterMotive
www.writermotive.co.uk

Wholeheartedly and devotedly
dedicated to

Lynn

my best friend, ally and confidante
who, I suspect, would have
approved and applauded

With thanks to:

Zara de Moira
For making my notes into words suitable to be published

Graham Middleton
For his editorial assistance

Sarah Partridge (SLB Creative Solutions)
For her fantastic cover design

Lesley Brown
For the use of her photographic talents

Disclaimer

The contents of this book are based on true circumstances and experiences.

Names and some details have been changed for privacy purposes, but the characters described are real people and the stories are recounted from actual events, although, obviously, told from a subjective point of view.

No offence is intended to anyone characterised here, neither is there any intention of making the characters recognisable from the descriptions or details given.

Contents

PREFACE

My name is David. I'm a landscape gardener by trade and I live in a quiet rural village in the south of England.

This book evolved from notes I made as I ventured into what was, for me, new and unfamiliar territory. It is offered and intended as a celebratory account of the many people I have met and enjoyed during this chapter of my life. It is also written in acknowledgement of the healing effect this journey has had on me. Indeed, this experience has been therapeutic on many levels and in ways I could not have predicted.

It is, perhaps, not the most orthodox therapy route but, whatever judgements may be made on its contents, if this book opens minds or offers hope to a fellow sufferer then that would be a bonus to add to the primary intention, which was to achieve a way forward for myself.

Before we begin, I feel I should provide some background to explain how and why I found myself in this position.

One chilly autumn day, not quite four years into my marriage, I moved into my current home, with my wife, blissfully happy to have found a place we both loved and with many plans for our future together there, only to have her almost immediately diagnosed with cancer. Horrible, hideously aggressive breast cancer. There followed an emergency double mastectomy and urgent treatment with chemotherapy but, despite a short-lived glimmer of hope and another dose of chemo, it became apparent that we were fighting a losing battle. As a last stand we tried radiotherapy but this sadly failed to gain us the control we were hoping for and the impact of these treatments, along with the disease itself, left Lynn ravaged and in constant pain.

In true heroic-patient style, she never complained, in fact she always said how lucky she felt. Tortured as I was, I had to question this attitude. Her reply was that, despite her life being cut short, she had been fortunate enough to have the opportunity to visit places and experience things that others might never see or experience in a lifetime. She was someone who was naturally inclined to gratitude rather than negativity. Certainly she was fairly well travelled and had lived an active and interesting life. However, I discovered that her perspective had also partly come from spending time in a hospital ward next to a young girl who had been told her cancer was terminal at the age of sixteen, long before so much of her life's future potential had a chance to blossom. This tragedy had a deep impact on Lynn's assessment of her own situation and this ability to see the bigger picture was one of the many, many reasons I loved her so incredibly much.

Always endeavouring to maintain a positive outlook, the only real regret she outwardly expressed, in a letter she wrote to me just before she died, was that she and I had had such a relatively short time together. We'd been married less than four years when the cancer made its presence known and turned our world on its head. Her subsequent operation and treatment meant that during the ten months and one day of her diagnosed illness we managed to piece together just three good weeks, all the while knowing that the chance of successful treatment and eventual remission was exceedingly slim. For the duration of her illness we constantly felt on borrowed time.

After a natural period of resistance and denial, the reality of the situation began insidiously to seep in. It had become apparent that the array of treatments Lynn had tried just hadn't worked and we were forced to accept that the disease was probably going to be fairly short and almost certainly terminal. The speed with which this horror story had unravelled left us both in shock. However, with acceptance and the end of intensive treatment, there seemed to come a period where Lynn felt almost well for a time. Desperately feeling the need to escape, we made arrangements to go abroad and visit her extended family in Canada during the short interim before the multitude of secondary tumours had a chance to properly take hold. It was a good move, giving us a chance to relax and enjoy each other's company in an environment where we were distracted from the menacing shadow lurking over us which, for so long, had been almost impossible to ignore or forget. I have such wonderful memories of our trip and am infinitely grateful to have had that opportunity.

Once home from Canada, the ever-practical Lynn set about organising her own funeral, almost seeming to get a new lease of life from the ability to move forward, despite it being in such a limited way. However, her health inevitably declined and in late August she was finally admitted to The Rowans Hospice just outside Portsmouth. Within a few days her condition began to deteriorate in that giveaway fashion that anyone who has witnessed it would recognise.

On the last day, I sat cradling her through her agitation and subsequent phases of morphine-induced calm while I gazed blindly at the endlessly open view beyond the window. Suddenly, without warning, I felt her grip on my hand tighten very strongly. Glancing down I was astounded to see her fully conscious and engaged, eyes sparkling and colour returned.

'Hello my darling' she said. 'Kiss me…'

I smiled, amazed to see and hear her like this, and happily obliged.

11

David B

One last kiss.

One last 'I love you'.

Moments later she lapsed back into semi-consciousness and shortly afterwards left me forever.

It was the culmination of a relatively short journey by some people's standards, which had taken me to despair and back so many times I was lost in a turmoil of intensely mixed emotions. Unacceptably, to my disbelieving mind, these included something that resembled relief that she was gone, purely to put an end to the physical and emotional agony which had plagued us both through these past months. It was a very natural, human response in the circumstances, I see that now, but at the time it pricked hard at my bewildered conscience that I could even have produced such a thought about my beloved girl.

On the day of the funeral, I bought her home in her self-chosen, simple coffin and we spent our very last hour together in her favourite part of the garden, whilst I picked flowers to accompany her on her journey. She had opted for a natural burial, clothed in her wedding dress, high on a hill with open views to the sea. I arranged to dig her grave myself, hoping that those hours of introspection and communing with her final resting place would bring some sense of closure, of resolution, even sanctuary maybe, but they did not. I was simply numbed with grief. I also performed the small, very private ceremony, playing songs she herself had chosen and prepared, dissipating into the air the last vestiges of her earthly presence.

My head understood by now that she was gone.

My heart did not, would not, could not accept it.

My memory of the first year after losing Lynn is hazy to say the least. Alcohol was my new partner of choice, imbibed to almost constant excess, with or without the company of whichever friends were prepared to join me for a time on my darkly painful journey. Desperately trying to distance myself from the reality of the situation I, more or less, abandoned my work, though I was fortunate to have good enough relationships with most of those who employed me for them to give me the space and understanding I needed to find my way through that stage.

Sometime around the six month point, on one of the few occasions when I'd managed to raise my head above water for more than a few hours at a time, I sought the advice of my doctor, luckily one who knows me fairly well. He talked to me at length before offering me some counselling sessions, which I resisted the idea of, or antidepressants if I wanted them, which I didn't. He considered the situation for a few moments but decided that, on the whole, he wasn't overly worried about me, feeling that this was all just part of the grieving process. However, he arranged to check in with me on a regular basis to monitor my progress, which was exactly what I really needed - a safety net, just in case. It was good judgement on his part and gave me the anchor point I needed while I continued my reluctant process of adjustment.

As the day of the first anniversary of Lynn's passing approached, things seemed to decline even further for a while. In practice it was just another day in the myriad of edgeless days filling that year of alcohol-dulled misery but somehow that first marking of a year gone by cut me so deeply, so cruelly, I could barely function.

Having made it, somehow, across the gaping chasm of that painful milestone, I continued as before for several more months, despairing of ever feeling a sense of normality again.

But, slowly, I began to surface and half-heartedly tried to piece a more regular existence back together, mainly by moderating my drinking a little and returning to work in stages. There were quite a few blips along the way but gradually, over months, some kind of a routine took shape and I, eventually, stuttered my way back to a point where I at least appeared to be holding things together again, albeit that this was largely a determined and superficial pretence. Still emotionally dazed, it was a pretty rudimentary existence at that time.

Despite this, in the closing stages of that year, still aching with the loss of Lynn but at least now functioning on a day-to-day level, I decided to go ahead with some work on restoration of the cottage, thinking it would serve as distraction with a purpose.

The house had needed complete renovation and that was something Lynn and I had planned to do gradually over several years. That plan was never started while we were there together, of course, however, when it transpired that after disbursements and despite my best efforts to drink my way through the better part of it, I had enough money from the insurances, etc, to restore the house in one go, I went ahead as it seemed like a positive thing to do, a sideways step forward of sorts.

There followed a tough year, but I was still in such a downhearted state I just ploughed on through, fairly indifferent to all the stress and inconvenience. I suppose it at least gave me something else to focus on for a time and thus I made it through to the following autumn, now two full years after Lynn's passing. I still was not happy by any means but at least managing my daily life in a tolerable way.

Once the project was complete, though, I found I missed having something to anchor my thoughts to and felt the need to replace it with something to help to divert my mind from its tendency to sink back into the murky depths.

Passing a local garden centre, I noticed a large banner outside advertising an end of season sale of hot tubs. It was not an idea I'd have dreamed up without seeing that banner but my attention was caught and, after some investigation, I decided it was the right choice. It felt like positive progress to me, an investment the hope that I might yet find some enjoyment in life. It gave me a way to quietly embrace a simple pleasure and it worked well on that level. Something I could enjoy on my own terms and which, as someone with a very physical job, had practical benefits too. It was an investment I have never regretted for a moment.

I had no inclination to socially engage with others in general as it still felt out of line with my state of mind. This suited me fine but my family were vocal in their concerns about my virtually non-existent social life and loud in their insistence that l should take more care of my health after my long sojourn in the realms of lethargy and alcohol abuse. Keen to get them off my case, I did give some thought to what avenues were on offer and, following up on a friend's suggestion, somewhat against my better judgement and despite suffering from two-left-feet syndrome, I decided to give modern jive dancing a try.

That turned out to be a good choice in the end since I could, without any self-consciousness, drop in on my own without needing to be reliant on anyone else nor to let anyone down if I was having a bad day and didn't feel up to going. Once there, I would slot into the rotating line of dancers where I would be presented with an ever-changing array of faces which felt social without the need for me to make a great deal of conversation. It was a bold move, which took my family by surprise as dancing was probably the last thing they would have expected me to do, but it abruptly stopped their nagging, which was a worthy result in its own right.

Actually, I found it suited me and, contrary to my expectations when I started, I stuck with it. Over the following months I began to feel less awkward with the dancing; in fact I began to actually enjoy it. Slowly, by default, rather than design, I got to know a whole lot of new people, several of whom have gone on to become good and close friends, proving their worth in many ways.

Eventually, still trying to normalise my life, I even tried out one or two potential relationships but they failed at early stages, well before the physical hurdle had been cleared. Despite a healthy sexual appetite I just couldn't engage emotionally with anyone whilst I was still so utterly in love with someone else, even if that person happened to be dead. Sex with someone who had an emotional investment in me didn't feel like an option when I knew I wasn't going to be able to reciprocate. My manly desires were thus thwarted.

It was now more than three years since I'd lost Lynn but I knew I truly was not ready to have any kind of romantic relationship. Well-meaning friends who were active on dating websites at that time constantly encouraged me to have a look and try it out but, uninspired, I would sit glumly at my screen scanning the ubiquitous lines of profile pictures, feeling like I might as well be from another planet. All I could see were rows of women who had the potential to give me a certain, much needed, release but whose requirement for emotional attachment could only be disappointed by my utter lack of ability to provide it. It was a tricky time, as my physical need was starting to make itself known pretty strongly, but the thought of starting a process where any woman was going to potentially want, even expect, to have a 'relationship' with me sent me scurrying for cover.

Fortunately, my social life had regained some momentum. In addition to the stalwart drinking companions of old, I now had my new-found dancing friends who had, with some acquired insight into my situation, seen fit to scoop me up and involve me in their social schedule. They were a lively bunch and I was rarely short of things to do if I was up to going out. I was starting to relax a little and enjoy my time with people more, though Lynn was never far from my thoughts. Occasionally, I would sink beneath the waves again and retreat for a time to regroup, but, fortunately, people were generally understanding of my situation, always keeping in touch but allowing me hibernation time when I needed it without taking it too personally.

Life went on, still something of an emotional rollercoaster at times but becoming more stable as the months went by. Although there was no let-up in the pain of loss I felt whenever Lynn crossed my mind, which was still often, I was by now having a happy social time, becoming increasingly close to my new group of friends. Feelings of affection for these people, especially some of the single women, made me wonder whether I might be getting closer to the possibility of considering a relationship, but the answer was always still no. Even after all this time, I just couldn't get my head around it. So I gave up and buried my thoughts, memories and burgeoning libido beneath a thick layer of social engagement.

Autumn loomed once more, that recurring dark cloud on my horizon, always threatening stormy weather and dismal prospects. I battened down the emotional hatches and did my best to dodge its menacing shadow as it passed over, taking with it the fourth anniversary of having a Lynn-shaped hole in the fabric of my life. Once through the inevitable turmoil, I paused, took a deep, determined breath and headed relentlessly on towards Christmas.

17

Christmas is not a great season for me as the gap always seems larger and deeper at that time of year. I shelved the demons as best I could and kept myself busy, endeavouring to maintain at least an outwardly buoyant facade.

I even found myself on the receiving end of some romantic attention from someone I'd met out dancing. Despite my ingrained tendency to automatically rebuff any advances, she persisted and we ended up going out on a few dates. Half thinking it might be possible that I could see a glimmer of light a long way down the tunnel, I began to open up to her and found myself wondering if there might be a glow of possibility here after all these years in the dark. She was good company, very empathetic and I was starting to feel a deeper attraction to her which filled me with equal parts of anticipation and trepidation. However, the light of potential was short-lived, being snuffed out by the realisation that she had been running our fledgling relationship alongside another long term one in addition to yet another flirtation which I learned about through a mutual friend. I scuttled back to my cave of celibacy feeling more than a little disheartened.

I survived Christmas and New Year more or less intact, breathed a sigh of relief and prepared to resume my usual routine. Quite unexpectedly, however, everything was about to change.

One afternoon in early January, a text arrived from a friend that spun me into a perplexed state. It read:

> 'Hi Dave, Happy New Year! Hope you got through Christmas ok and managed to have a good time. I know some of it will have been difficult for you. I'm struggling a little myself, as you know. I have a bit of a personal question for you. Forgive me for asking, but I just wondered if you might be up

for a bit of, ummm, mutual physical therapy, if you know what I mean? I know you
don't want a relationship with anyone and
neither do I but there is one thing I do kind
of need... There aren't many guys I know
well enough to even suggest this to or trust
enough to approach (can't quite believe I'm
writing this at all actually). If it's not something you're interested in then that's absolutely fine, of course. Either way, I'd be
grateful if you didn't mention this to anyone. Let me know what you think x'

I read and re-read the message a few times, trying to make
sure I'd got the gist of it right. Then I poured myself a glass
of wine and read it once more. When I was quite certain that
she'd meant what I thought she meant, I sat and contemplated the prospect for a while. It wasn't something I'd been in
any way prepared for and I was a bit blown away to be honest. I couldn't decide how I felt about it. She was an attractive girl and on that basis I was up for it, enthusiastic even,
but I wasn't experienced in the area of 'friends with benefits'
and I was also wary of lighting the fuse to a potential time
bomb on the wider edge of a group of friends whose company I enjoyed and, by this stage, rather relied on. As the
spectrum of reactions continued to play through my mind I
became suddenly concerned that my delay in responding
might seem rude in the circumstances. I thought I'd better
make a decision one way or another, so, I sent her a reply
which I hoped might convey the appropriate mix of enthusiasm and caution. I then poured a second glass of wine and
stood at the kitchen window, watching the rain beating mercilessly down on the garden whilst trying to absorb this new
proposition.

What was funny, in the end, was how perturbed I'd been and
how concerned I was to word my response correctly when,

19

within a short space of time, back bounced a very matter of fact message from her saying that she was glad I was open to the idea and wondering if perhaps we could get together later that same evening.

My brain did a sort of sideways shift at that. This new concept which had taken me by surprise and which I wasn't sure I'd fully adjusted to, was now threatening to materialise imminently. But, then again, I am a man and there aren't too many men who would baulk at the idea of an attractive woman contacting him and offering him sex purely for mutual fulfilment with no strings attached. It seemed almost too good to be true and I did wonder if there was an ulterior motive in place but, on balance, I decided I was prepared to take a chance. Steeling myself, I invited her over to mine that evening, making it clear that if she changed her mind that was fine, she could just come for a drink anyway.

I think I expected that she would probably back out and find she couldn't go through with it but I had underestimated her on that. When she arrived, I offered her a drink but she just smiled and declined. 'You sure you want to do this?' I asked. Her response was calm and self-assured. A definite yes. So we bypassed the wine, headed straight upstairs, undressed and hopped into bed. It felt quite surreal in some senses but a part of me was suddenly jubilant. Finally, I had discovered a situation where the prospect of sex so close at hand hadn't sent me into an instant decline. It had to be the lack of emotional pressure, ties and on-going commitments. It was just sex for its own sake, pure and unadulterated.

Eureka!

We ended up having a mutually satisfying time together after which we sat for a little while and had a glass of wine before she headed off to some dance event or other and I was left alone to chew over what had just occurred. I had the impression that it was going to be a one-off from her point of view although I'd made it crystal clear that I'd be more than happy to oblige if she felt the need again.

For my part, I was just struck by the simplicity of it all. Two people with a common need fulfilling that need together and then moving on. It was so...easy. Contrary to my concerns, after the initial awkwardness I had found that it seemed perfectly natural and fine. My mind and body were still blissfully reverberating with the relief of co-enjoyed physical release after so long roaming the sexual desert.

I felt poised on the edge of a new domain but wasn't really sure how to move forward. It was one thing a woman propositioning a male friend in that way but I couldn't see it working in reverse. In fairness, even if that had been acceptable I'm not sure I even knew enough women to cope with the tidal wave of need which I suspected would break forth once I opened my floodgates. One thing was for certain, I needed sex, just sex, preferably lots of it and as soon as possible.

Inevitably, I arrived back at the banal, unappealing prospect of attempting to instigate a relationship with someone. I could almost hear the whirring of my sexual engines cease at the instant I had the thought. 'Come on', I directed myself, firmly, 'four and a half years is just too long to wallow like this'. So I sat down once more at my PC and opened the long-dormant list of dating website pages once again.

A smiling sea of faces greeted me and I began listlessly to scan them, row after row, occasionally clicking on one but rapidly retreating every time. Eventually, all but losing the will to live, I closed them down and trailed dejectedly up to bed.

21

A day or two later, when the afterglow of my unexpected visit had worn off and my physical needs were making themselves felt with renewed vigour, I determined to give the websites another go. Yet again, I sat flicking through endless pages until, by chance, in a discreet corner of the screen, I spotted something that finally sparked my interest. It was an advert for an 'adult-fun' website. A dating website without the dating, so to speak.

One click, a quick look around and a tentative profile later, my hopes had been lifted and a crusade, of sorts, was underway.

* * * * *

Anyone reading this book will naturally make their own judgements of one kind or another but please try to keep an open mind. The extreme nature of my choice of therapy should not deter you from acknowledging its potential, even if it is not something you wish to try yourself, nor should it detract from your enjoyment of the purely entertaining aspects of the various episodes I have chosen to recount. My encounters have provided me with new perspectives which eventually, though by no means immediately, lifted me from my reverie and helped me leave behind my prolonged, soul-numbing, grief. In my case, these experiences have resulted in an ability to find a renewed sense of something approaching contentment within the confines of a situation that was thrust most unwillingly upon me. They have also provided a platform from which I feel I have the potential to move forward from what, for a long time, had been an almost terminally static position. It may or may not be the final answer but it has been part of the evolutionary process of my life. Whilst I'm reluctant to speculate on where the process will take me next, I feel pretty content with where it has taken me thus far.

I have not written this intending to glamourise or glorify the lifestyle, nor to recommend it as a suitable therapy for all. Neither would I suggest that it is something you, yourself, should necessarily try, but I hope to broaden your mind as well as, I hope, to entertain you, as I have, indeed, been so thoroughly entertained myself.

I wish you an enjoyable read.

David

ps. As an aside, I should express that during these encounters I have maintained as rigorous attention as possible to protecting myself and to practicing safe sex. I have not made much reference to this fact in the writing, not wishing to punctuate your reading flow with such mundanity, so I will make that rather practical point here and leave it at that.

David B

Getting No Satisfaction

With not much concept of what to expect from 'adult fun' (or swinging), I made a tentatively hopeful start into this new domain. One the one hand, I suppose I had half an idea that, with little effort on my part, veritable hordes of gloriously highly-sexed women would be soon hurling themselves in my direction, weak with gratitude at my manly fulfilment of their desires and undemanding of my input on any other level. Of course, I rapidly became aware of the fact that it doesn't quite work like that.

Conversely, like most people, I also had in the back of my mind a few of the standard notions of it being primarily the prowling realm of subversive nymphomaniacs and potential psychopaths, but I tried to put those thoughts out of my head. As it turns out, my experiences so far have not thrown many, or, in fact, any psychotically disturbed people into my path but perhaps I have just been lucky. I daresay there are a few of them out there if you care to look or are unlucky.

Having steeled myself to be so bold as to actually create a profile, I sat in anticipation of, well, something happening at least. Feeling somewhat sheepish for embarking on this quest at all, I was half expecting to be struck down by the lightning bolt of God's own fury for having dared to even consider it, however, my relief at said lightning bolt's non-appearance soon faded, only to be replaced within twenty four hours with slight disappointment that nothing else had occurred either. Not so much as a single message. In fact, there had been no response of any kind at all, from anyone, to my gleaming new profile.

I pondered this problem at length before deciding that I'd been foolish to expect such a rapid response and that patience and aloofness were plainly what was required. I was sure I'd read or heard somewhere that hunting a woman was like hunting a wild animal; it required stealth, patience and confidence. Well, if that's what was needed, I was sure I could sit this one out. The Waiting Game. The Hunter and The Hunted. I was pretty certain I could wait as long as it took.

Reluctantly, after another twenty-four more finger-tapping hours, I had to acknowledge that perhaps, in this situation anyway, patience was a virtue I possessed in pitifully inadequate quantities. My affronted mind invented all manner of reasons for the resounding silence currently inhabiting my inbox, ultimately concluding that they were all out there, those women, probably in conspiratorial cahoots, just waiting for me to make the first move.

So I scanned the list of profiles showing currently available single ladies who were actively looking for a 'date'. Picking out a rather stunning looking woman whose provocative profile picture stance seemed to give a pretty good impression of what she was after, I composed a message which I hoped would convey my willingness and ability to please her mixed with some positive comments about her appearance. Regrettably, my message tailed off into something which, reading it back the next day, came across almost as an apology for wasting her valuable time as, by then, I had lapsed into a mild crisis of confidence and was almost mortified at my own audacity for daring to write to her at all.

Perhaps not surprisingly, I didn't get a response to that message. Determined to persevere and put the lessons learned into practice, I tried again with a different profile. And again with another. By the end of the week I had sent out seven or eight messages without a single response. Going for broke,

25

that night I sent out messages to around ten different women.

I suspect, looking back, that if I'd had no response to any of those messages either I'd have been inclined to give up but I did, in fact, get responses from two of the ladies, one almost immediate and one a day or two later. Things progressed to a degree with each of them and although neither encounter quite worked out as I had planned, which I will elaborate on in a moment, in the aftermath I simply had to decide that I had learned valuable lessons which would, no doubt, serve me well in the future.

As with standard dating sites, the profiles that people create can be misleading, sometimes wantonly so, to the point of them being abject works of fiction. The filtering process becomes easier with experience but there is always the potential for the peruser to be utterly duped. Some people have no ethical boundaries on this and don't seem to get the fact that an honest profile is more likely to lead to a successful meet in the long run. I also suspect that some people are fundamentally more than a little deluded about their own self-image.

There are some general precautionary tactics one picks up along the way which help to avoid time wasting and disappointment. It is, like anything, a learning process and I went through that process in several stages. Generally, the first precaution is to get together with a prospective partner for the first time in a public place (a bar or cafe, for example). An initial interview, if you like, to assess, on both sides, the potential for progression without undue assumptions being made or any awkwardness if either party decides against proceeding further. The second is to decide where your own boundaries are, although this, of course, is something you mainly discover along the way by default as the potential candidates present themselves and you feel an automatic yes or no reaction.

Of course, for any of those precautions to be relevant you have to get to the point of having made contact and agreed to meet with someone in the first place, no mean feat it seemed in those early days. One very important lesson I learned as I went along was that it's as much how you say it as what you say and that less can definitely be more. But more of that later.

It is a different world, a parallel universe of sorts, which is secretly interwoven into the fabric of daily life, unnoticed by most but seething away in the gaps between our personal realities, whilst we go about our daily grind, oblivious. When consciously experienced, it rapidly opens your eyes wide once you realise just how much goes on, sometimes no more than a hair's breadth beneath the awareness of the uninitiated. An extra-curricular world in which it helps to prepare yourself mentally, so far as possible, for any eventuality, where it pays to expect the unexpected. A world where open-mindedness is not only a virtue but an absolute necessity.

My developing formula, over the first few weeks and months, evolved into a routine that seemed to cover most bases. Firstly, as a rule, there would be a casual meet on neutral territory. If, after meeting, there appeared to be a positive ambience and I thought I might like to take things further I would suggest a rendezvous at my place on the basis that it would be a relaxed environment, free from potential disturbances, in a discreet location. If the contact was a single lady then I would always offer to cook as this seemed to set the scene and make the whole thing seem a bit more natural, less forced.

Until I got fully embedded in this lifestyle, I found that making a little bit of an effort was a good way to adjust my mind by stages to this new scenario, one where I needed to re-learn the rule book. It did take a bit of getting used to. As time went on, I needed that element less but I still found it

27

preferable to enhance the environment at least a little, where possible. It stopped it all feeling too clinical and faceless and, of course, you can never be absolutely certain exactly what frame of mind your erstwhile partner might be in, so I feel it's best to be prepared, just in case.

Another reason for hosting meets at my home was Milton. Loyal, devoted Milton, my lovely old, mercifully non-judgemental Wolfhound, who, advanced in years as he was, required a bit more attention than your average dog and wouldn't have thanked me for staying out late and leaving him unattended for any great length of time. He was a big, friendly mountain of a dog and seemed to enjoy all these new people turning up. Well, most of them anyway. My faith in him as a judge of human character grew increasingly over the time he was welcoming these visitors to our home and in the end I almost felt that the level of his welcome gave some indication of the likely success of the meet, although, on occasion, his forceful greetings looked more likely to send some poor dog-wary damsel straight back out the door before I'd had much of a chance to get fully acquainted.

Through trial and error, I refined my formula along the way, adapting ideas as I made my mistakes. For example, I very quickly realised that this could become quite an expensive hobby as my preference would be to cook a decent meal, from scratch, using high quality ingredients and with a decent bottle of wine. Too expensive, perhaps, it occurred to me, after only my second meet.

Miss V, from Basingstoke, was one of the two ladies who had responded to my multi-target message effort. She came for dinner on a Saturday night after an initial midweek meet, which I felt had gone pretty well. She was perhaps a little strident in her manner for my taste but that was something I was happy to overlook for the period of a brief encounter. She had sat in my kitchen with a nice glass of wine, chatting away cheerfully enough while I finished off the cooking. She appeared to heartily enjoy the meal I had painstakingly prepared, courtesy of Waitrose, M&S & the local farmers market, along with a £12 bottle of Pinot Grigio. Once replete, however, she rose from the table and announced, without thanks or apology, that she had to go, sweeping out and disappearing into the night leaving me speechlessly bewildered in her wake.

I suppose she must have had her reasons, perhaps it was all too much and she just wanted me to get on with the job! It would have been nicer, though, if she'd chosen to share her thoughts rather than just abandon the mission.

Perhaps I should explain that I always endeavour to eat and drink well myself but the Miss V experience left me wondering why I should cook a fresh organic fillet of salmon for someone who likely wouldn't appreciate it and who was quite within her rights to just up and go after being fed and watered. So, with that in mind, I started to shop at better value supermarkets for cheaper packs of frozen salmon or meat and less expensive wine. I have found that most people seem to prefer red wine whilst I enjoy white more, so if someone turns up who is a red wine drinker (ascertained on the initial meet) then I will have prepared in advance by decanting el cheapo vino into an impressive bottle which once held a very fine red wine, given to me by a work client one Christmas. Not one person has ever given me the impression that they had the faintest idea they were drinking an inferior wine, I honestly don't believe most people would know the difference anyway. It is a little bit of a grey area, I admit, but it seemed a suitable compromise at the time. Certainly, my efforts do seem to help create a sense of occasion, which proved to be generally conducive to a satisfactory outcome.

Manipulating the food element can be slightly more difficult as my preferred wild salmon has a very obvious colour difference when compared with the farmed variety I was dishing up for my 'date'. However, the colour difference diminishes on cooking and I have so far managed to get away without so much as a hint that any of my delightful lady friends have suspected a thing. I am left-handed so I simply keep my fillet on the left of the pan and the lady is none the wiser. I sometimes feel a little awkward when, during the meal, my guest says 'this is delicious...' and I sheepishly admit to myself, yes, but not as delicious as mine. I hope this does not sound too harsh, I am just a man on a budget trying to keep unappreciated expenditure to a minimum. I would like to think that I have never served anything which was not tasty and enjoyable in its own right, regardless of comparison with my alternative.

Would I get away with it on *Come Dine With Me*?

Probably not.

I Saw Her Face, But I Shouldn't Believe Her

Having had some initial interaction with the standard world of online dating, I was, as I have mentioned, already aware of the fictional elements which can creep into people's profiles. Having then sidestepped into 'adult fun' dating, I very soon discovered that the same applied here too. As a starry-eyed newcomer, however, I'd pretty much taken everything at face value and assumed that the profiles I saw were essentially a similarly full and honest description of the person concerned as I had endeavoured to produce for mine. Subconsciously, I suppose I felt that surely in a zone where people were being so open about what they wanted there was no need for being dishonest about other elements of a profile. Looking back, I can't believe I didn't foresee that this perception was so naive and so flawed.

On my mass messaging mission, a mission which I largely suspected would be an abject failure and the ultimate demise of my failed-to-launch swinging career, I had carefully written a generic message which I could adapt fairly easily to suit the recipient. I then simply fired them off to any seemingly suitable candidates who caught my eye with all the abandon of a man with nothing to lose.

Of the two responses I had to those messages, the first came from the very last email I sent that evening. It was from 'Miss M' from Wokingham, a seemingly blameless angel with a perfect profile and a very pretty photograph. Of her face. Just her face. I honestly suspected nothing. In fact, I would

31

go so far as to say that, in some ways, hers was probably the profile I'd found most appealing of all.

After my customary moments of hovering over the 'send' button, I had despatched the message on its way with a wretchedly low level of expectation, my head almost hanging in shame at my own unworthy presumption.

To my utter delight, a return message pinged back within minutes. This immediacy was a truly heart-warming relief to the ego and sent my self-esteem flying straight back in the opposite direction. Buoyed up by this newfound state of swoon-worthy attractiveness (which I now, naturally, imagined I possessed) I had returned the compliment. Messages bounced back and forth and by the end of the evening we had exchanged mobile phone numbers and were texting avidly. Within days we had arranged to meet and I girded my loins for my first foray into the beautiful world of no-strings sex with undemanding, hot, horny Babestation wannabes.

It was a Wednesday and the traffic was dreadful. I arrived, eventually, in Wokingham flustered and late, desperately hoping that my unavoidable tardiness would not dent the ardour of my delicious newfound playmate. She was due to have arrived by train some twenty minutes prior to my late arrival so, having located the designated meeting place, I stood in full sight, anxiously scanning the station for any sign of Miss M's presence.

Irritatingly, my view was somewhat blocked by the advancing mass of a Sherman tank poorly disguised as human female. Tutting and huffing my frustration as I tried to peer round her, it eventually crossed my mind to wonder why the hell she wasn't getting out of my way. The penny finally dropped.

Now, I don't wish to sound shallow and I am, in fact, an appreciative fan of the curvy female form, but, frankly, the sudden realisation that the Divine Miss M was, in fact, Miss Monstrously Misleading Mountain of a Munter with Minimal Morals and a Manipulative Mentality left me momentarily in shock. Unable to string a coherent thought process together I capitulated when she suggested we decamp to a nearby pub, exceedingly keen, as I was, to find any less conspicuous location than the one we currently occupied. Looking back, I should have just made my apologies, turned tail and left there and then, but I appear to suffer with an affliction of manners in these situations and it would have seemed too rude to do so, despite her obvious and shameless effort at, if not out and out deception then certainly an unforgivable economy with the truth. The head shot she'd used for her profile was plainly years out of date and from a time before she had grown to her current proportions.

Her choice of venue was a pub named The Three Frogs. I couldn't help thinking that The Three Pigs (and their bloody big sister) would have been a more appropriate name, and I was muttering these thoughts to myself as I skulked through the door whilst trying, and sadly failing, to make myself invisible.

The looks I got were interesting, ranging from plain disgust to something approaching awe! Yes, I'm not just being a drama queen, she actually was that big. Big enough to be quite a spectacle. A look which was further enhanced when she ordered and proceeded to work her way through a virtual mountain of food: a mixed grill platter with extra fries and numerous side orders which she consumed with gusto, occasionally, for the trickier bits, even availing herself of the cutlery provided.

Not being a person who enjoys this kind of attention, I was left helplessly drowning in an ocean of self-consciousness. By the time she finished I was more than ready to leave but, rather masochistically, couldn't resist hanging on for a few more minutes while I won a bet I'd made with myself that Miss Munchwagon would NOT be able to resist the two or three chips she had left at the side of her plate. I didn't have to wait long before leaving the pub victorious in at least that small way, escaping home a wiser man after, as politely as possible, denying her request for another meet.

She didn't let up straight away either, messaging me several times requesting dates and suggesting play themes which frankly had me shaking my head in wonder at her delusions. I doubt that a person of her stature could actually achieve some of the manoeuvres she was putting forward as supposedly alluring suggestions, not without causing serious bodily injury to either herself or her playmate anyway. I'm over six feet tall and though not heavily built I have a physical job which means I'm reasonably strong and feel manfully capable in most situations, but I shuddered at the thought of contact sports with the Monstrous Miss M and was vastly relieved when she eventually interpreted my silence correctly, gave up and left me alone.

It wasn't the most encouraging of starts and, frankly, would have been quite enough of an experience in its own right to deter the faint-hearted. I must admit, it caused me to question the wisdom of pursuing this any further. However, although I didn't know at the time that my second meet, at home with Miss V, would prove to be the abortive mission it was, I am still grateful to them both for putting themselves forward at all since without having that perceived potential to motivate me to continue, I suspect I might have given it up as a fool's errand there and then.

I would have missed out on so much if I had.

Looking For Some Hot Tub, Baby, This Evening?

Although the purchase of my hot tub a couple of years earlier had perhaps seemed a little impetuous at the time, I had quickly come to the conclusion that it had been a worthy investment. I would often find myself out there in the garden with a restorative glass of wine, floating about in the soothing bubbles, enjoying the evening as the sun went down and the stars slowly appeared above my head. However, it had a future potential I could not have begun to imagine at the time I bought it and I would later grow to appreciate just how well it would serve me, proving itself, in many ways, to be one of the best purchasing decisions I have ever made. My single life gave me ample opportunity to enjoy the tub on a regular basis. However, as I embarked on the adult fun scene, I discovered unanticipated benefits in that it added greatly to my new venture on several levels.

When I message new prospects, I often mention that I have a hot tub and there is no question in my mind that it lends a great element of appeal. I would say that at least half of the encounters which I've hosted at home utilise the tub and, once there, almost invariably will progress to sex. It's a great ice-breaker as well as a very palatable way of getting through the 'clothes off' stage. The combination of hot water and slippery naked skin is an alluring and potent one. At any time of the year, an open view of the night sky is an inspiring sight, although in winter the low temperatures can take its toll on water-bound playtimes in certain positions. But, hey, you live and learn and the experimenting is always great fun.

I am pretty meticulous about maintaining the water and cleanliness, of course. I wouldn't want to risk a build-up of anything unpleasant and the thought of that having even the smallest chance to accumulate is very unappealing, but I use the tub all the time, whether alone or in company, so, for my own peace of mind, I monitor it almost daily and am perfectly happy that it's always in good shape.

When I find myself alone in there these days, not only is it a relaxing and enjoyable place to while away some time, but now, of course, I have countless, fun-filled memories to look back on and indulge in and it is never long before I am smiling away to myself remembering the details of some historical encounter or other.

I honestly have no idea exactly how many women I have become carnally acquainted with over the duration of this project. However, to the best of my remembered knowledge, I believe I messaged something like one hundred and twenty profiles, which in turn resulted in around sixty to seventy meets, so it's been about a fifty/fifty conversion rate at that level. Additionally, there were those who contacted me first, some of which also converted to meets and onward progression but suffice to say there are quite a number of bi-experimental couples and also bi-curious males who want to explore in safety without finding themselves in a situation they can't easily escape from. Whilst I can see how that might work well, I can honestly say none of those kinds of offers or suggestions has remotely tempted me as I'm totally straight and don't feel experimentally inclined about that at all, so I've backed off from quite a few approaches on that basis.

Obviously, not all meets progress to immediate sex or even to future play dates but I've found that over two thirds of my first meets progress to full encounters, so somewhere in the region of forty to fifty partners would be my best estimate.

There are many factors which influence this rate, not least the number of false profiles tucked away amongst the genuine ones. These might have been set up for any number of reasons from concealed advertising, which becomes apparent fairly quickly when you view the profile, to the voyeurs who simply get a kick out of eyeing up the possibilities but have no intention of interacting, to the picture scouts whose prime motive is purely to elicit personal, usually pornographic, photos from their targets. You do learn to spot these with experience but in the early days I did end up wasting a bit of time with them, one way or another.

Swinging, for me, simply offered a way to express and fulfil my physical needs without the pressure of having to deal head on with all those emotions I wasn't ready to confront and without the risk of misleading or causing pain to anyone in the process. Living this lifestyle as a single person can, for me, have a downside of slight feelings of loneliness at times, especially when I see friends happy with their partners. Although I am not against the idea of having a committed relationship again, or even the possibility of marriage at some point in the future, at this time there doesn't appear to be much prospect of that happening imminently and, for now, I am happy with the current balance of things

What has changed, though, is the fact that if a potential relationship presented itself I am now in a position to consider it an option. The passing of time is a great healer in its own right, of course, but the liberating experiences of the past eighteen months or so are, ironically enough, what has aided my progress in this area the most. The freedom of access to so many uninvolved relationships has ultimately, I believe, brought me round to feeling at least the potential ability to focus on a single, committed one.

Looking back over the array of encounters that colour this era of my life, I have tried to pick out and describe some of the key ones, good and bad, to give an impression of the full spectrum of what one might expect from a foray into the wonderful world of swinging. Not that I'm selling it as something everyone should be doing, not, in fact, that I wish to sell it at all, but as someone who considers himself game for an adventure but a fairly regular guy on the whole, my intention is to give similarly uninitiated individuals a little window on a world they might not have come across or might be toying with the idea of but have yet to take the plunge into.

I also felt the desire to share some of these stories as, when I embarked on this journey, I really could not have foreseen the sheer range of experiences I would have, from the bizarrely surreal to the comically entertaining to the mutually fulfilling and, occasionally the emotionally touching. Personally, I've pretty much loved every minute, despite the occasional low point, and look back with great amusement and affection over this period of my history in its entirety.

Back In The Saddle

Undeniably, creating an eye-catching profile is a key factor in attracting the right kind of attention. However, when you set up your profile and give the usual information: physical details, preferences, availability, etc, as I had already discovered, aside from their own, often seemingly absent, ethical boundaries, there's nothing to stop anyone putting any old thing on their profile on order to lure potential playmates into the fold under false pretences?

Happily, with swinging sites there is an integral, self-policing system of 'Verifications'. This works in much the same way as, for example, an online retailer's feedback rating. It is a system which works fairly effectively once you get started, although it is not rigorously enforced and most websites give you the opportunity to choose whether the feedback you are given is visible on your profile or not. Every meet results in a verification opportunity for both parties but you can manipulate the overall impression given to people viewing your profile by just deleting or not displaying the comments you don't like.

It cuts both ways, I suppose. You can block people's remarks if, perhaps, you've had a meet that didn't quite go according to plan and the other party has been unfair, but it's just a bit too easy to hide comments and deny visitors to your profile the opportunity to make a fair judgement, especially if you are finding that you need to block quite a bit of your feedback.

On your personal information alone, even with lots of pictures, the chances of achieving a satisfactory meet, or, in fact, any meets at all, appear to be really quite minimal. In order to make your profile appealing and effective you ideally need to have the all-important verifications. It comes across as a bit of a catch-22 to start with but I suppose it filters out those who are taking it seriously from those who are just on the site taking a look around or trying their luck.

The problem lies in the fact that, obviously, you need a successful first encounter to start you on the verification path and it began to seem like a bit of a challenge too far for a while in those early days. Later, with experience and after having done a fair bit of late night research into which profiles had the best lists of verifications and why that might be, I realised where I was, to some degree, going wrong but in the early stages I was still feeling my way along in the dark and had a lot to learn.

A few more weeks of getting 'no thanks' replies or, most often, no reply at all to messages I had sent out made getting those critical first verifications a mission in its own right for me. I was getting nowhere fast and came to the conclusion that a certain lowering of standards was going to be necessary in order to move things along. It was a slightly worrying chance to take but in the end I decided that it just had to be done so, having had a firm word with myself, I began a half-hearted trawl through the less desirable prospects. Holding my instinctive responses hard in check, I eventually decided on a couple, 'Mr & Mrs G', whose profile seemed to be the least unappealing of a bad bunch. Battling against my better judgement, I despatched a short message, half hoping that it too would be ignored and spare me the need to follow through.

The following day I had a reply. It was not exactly eloquent but it was benignly welcoming and instigated a conversation that, within days, led me to arrange a meet with them. They were in their late fifties, seemed friendly enough and their messages simply said that they were experiencing a certain staleness in their sex life after twenty five years of marriage and wanted to inject a bit of variety. No face shots were available of either of them, just a couple of random body shots so I didn't have a great deal to go on to prepare myself, although there was plenty of scope to imagine the worst. Suffice to say, my expectations were low. Regardless of this, however, armed with their limited profile information and a determined, if slightly wary, attitude, I took a deep breath and embarked into the fray.

I invited them to my house, where I felt on safer ground, on what had turned out to be a dreary, wet Friday afternoon in February. As the hour of the meet relentlessly approached, I admit I was becoming more and more apprehensive. What on earth was I doing? I asked myself repeatedly. But I couldn't very well bail at this late stage, I decided, pacifying my now hyperactive imagination with the thought that if I really couldn't go through with it I'd just have to send them on their way with a couple of drinks and hope they didn't mind too much or take it personally.

After the Miss M scenario, I'd deliberated for a long while over having an initial meet with this couple but had decided that it might be best not to know too much of what to expect in advance, just jump straight in and get it over with. So, here I was, perched on the edge of my sofa, anxiously twisting my second glass of wine in agitated hands wondering if, with all this tension, come the moment I was going to be able to get it up at all. I confess my heart was racing a bit, the edge of my comfort zone now having been left far behind.

At length, I heard them at the door, and, after wavering for a moment I went, with trepidation, to let them in and greet my destiny. As I'd expected, the lady was no stunner, but, forc-

41

ing myself to be objective, she had a reasonably nice, curvy body with plenty to play with up top. Choosing to focus on this somewhat limited point of appeal, I proceeded to imbibe alcohol to a level where my primary selective faculties were suitably dulled.

There had been little by way of verifications on their profile, as they too were fairly new to the scene. However, they seemed much more comfortable with the situation than I felt and I was surprised, given their limited experience, at just how unperturbed they were in the face of this encounter. After an affable but fairly brief chat, they made it clear they were keen to motor things along. Downing the remains of my wine I suggested we head to the bedroom and, before I had a chance to gather my senses, I'd been swept upstairs, stripped and prepared for the sacrifice.

In the context of this fascinating yet almost horrifyingly real situation, the alcohol proved to have been a good plan, eventually spreading a rather audaciously gung-ho attitude over my previous anxiety which had me embracing the moment with something approaching levity. Perhaps it was the adrenaline, perhaps the unfamiliarity of the scenario but I found myself being quite jocular, playful even, especially with Mrs G's upper regions, which were really quite entertaining in a voluminous, saucy kind of way. She put me in mind of a 'Carry On' film type of character, which amused me, although I kept the thought to myself.

I was relieved to find that Mr G, as had been suggested in their profile, was happy to keep a voyeuristic distance and made no attempt to get physically involved in the encounter, making his presence felt with his verbal input instead. I was feeling quite light-headed and was happy to just go with the flow while Mr G kept up an informative commentary in the style of a sports commentator, or possibly an auctioneer. Under his direction, I soon found myself merrily bouncing away on top of Mrs G, my slightly wine-befuddled mind rather perturbed to observe that her mountainous breasts had slid off to either side and were now pooled comfortably under her armpits. I was momentarily mesmerised watching their slack surfaces rippling in time with my own movements.

I suspect the alcohol also added to my sense of the surreal in the latter stages of our encounter as things took on a subtle resemblance, at points, to the final furlong of the bloody Grand National. My mount was no filly but there were certainly wild eyes and flared nostrils. She was also frisky enough to throw in some impressive bucks along the way, almost unseating me once or twice. Endeavouring to put in the winning performance as jockey, I began to understand the tendency these individuals have for getting the whip out when the finish line simply isn't coming fast enough. Perhaps it was just as well I did not have a whip to hand. Certainly, if we'd had a bookie in the room I reckon he'd have been offering some pretty long odds on us finishing the race at all, but the cheering crowd, in this case taking the form of the rather portly Mr G, was reassuringly enthusiastic in support, offering loud whoops of encouragement and instructive advice in the closing stages, my favourite of which was:

'Stick your finger up her arse, mate, she loves that.'

This was casually thrown in amongst the rather more demure 'G'wan mate, really give it some' and 'YEAH..! Fuck 'er, mate, fuck 'er good...'

Well!

Eventually, my ride, with much snorting and whinnying, juddered her way into the winner's enclosure and at last I could dismount, exhausted, to receive hearty congratulations from her proud owner and trainer.

David B

As first swinging experiences go, fair to say this one was something of an eye-opener but it achieved the main objective and obtained for me my coveted first verification. It's perhaps easy to see why it can be tricky to get started.

Two Ain't A Magic Number

With the first verification down, it felt like I was making progress at last and I pursued my quest for further meets with a little more optimism. I managed to get a few responses which led on to a couple of meets over the following month or so, one of which, an older single lady, progressed to a full encounter, meaning that after several months of effort I had ended up with a grand total of two encounters and two corresponding verifications on my profile. It was most definitely not the open season sex-fest I'd been hoping for and if I could have come up with a suitable alternative I really think at this point I would have done so. Regardless of the two positive verifications on my profile, most of my messages were still not getting any response, which I found rather puzzling and exceedingly frustrating.

I confess that I had become a little bit addicted to the website and would spend time online, looking through profiles, during most of the spare moments I had in the day, logging in anywhere I could find an internet connection. I often stayed up into the night reading through the endlessly fascinating and seemingly infinite range of profiles, all different but all wanting, essentially, one thing. Well, the genuine ones, anyway. I was aware that my singular focus on this mission had got a bit out of hand but it was so compulsive, perusing the array of entries, knowing that many of them had the potential to lead me on another little adventure. Eventually, though, the same old profiles cropping up over and over, was becoming less entertaining and more frustrating. So I took a step back, limiting the time I spent scanning the site and logging in less often and finding that there were then, generally, a few new profiles to check out each time.

45

I felt that my mind-set had adjusted to the parameters of this new world and I was feeling pretty relaxed and comfortable with the concept although, so far, I hadn't been faced with anything particularly challenging or out of the ordinary. Not that I wanted anything like that, but I'd read through enough profiles to know that many people on this scene were likely to have predilections I perhaps hadn't encountered before. I was glad to have got at least to this stage without having been put on the spot or feeling out of my depth. The prospect of pursuing this lifestyle suited me just fine in principle, if only I could just speed the process up a little.

Frustration at the lack of progress made me consider ways I could broaden the range of potential suitors. I had looked at other websites and thought about signing up but since my hard-won verifications were both listed on the site I was already using, that idea didn't seem to offer much prospect of improvement. I also thought about extending the boundaries of my interests and range of acceptability, effectively inventing a new part of myself to accommodate some things I'd seen on other profiles which might open the options up a bit. After some consideration, I decided that being submissive might be something I could tolerate. I fired off a couple of messages to people whose profiles said they were looking for that scenario but who didn't appear too hard-core. I had responses to both messages and these made it immediately clear to me, in their different ways, that this was not going to be the easy fix I'd hoped for. A little further research confirmed that the sub/dom scene is a whole different ball-game and much as I was settling quite well into some new ways of thinking, I definitely wasn't ready for any of that.

I did feel mighty keen to initiate another successful encounter though and while I was pondering ways in which I might be able to achieve that I decided to do some more research into profile popularity. I spent an evening or two just comparing profiles, trying work out what the differences were

and why some might be more successful at attracting attention than others. Once I'd started looking objectively, it
didn't take long before I came to the sudden realisation that I
was just being too darned nice! Plainly still stuck in my old
thought patterns, it was suddenly obvious that adapting these
was key to making that essential and definitive step forward.
It still felt a bit alien to me to be putting myself out there in
this way but I decided I was going to have to bite the bullet
and bite it hard. My profile was just too innocuous. Too soft.
It was probably giving out a true representation of who I was
in the real world but that was not really what these people
wanted to know. So, what did they want to know? And what
impression should I be trying to give? In the early hours of
the following morning, after much consideration, a bottle or
more of wine and having forced my mind to cross the divide
and think from the perspective of a 'swinger', I narrowed
down my now obviously rambling profile to just a few
words:

> 'Professional single guy seeks similar female
> who fucks like a rabbit and sucks like a Dy-
> son'.

'Excellent', I thought, feeling that deep sense of victory you'd
expect of a rather drunk person on satisfactory completion
of a critically important mission. I rounded off my new image with a couple of less standard-issue photos, including
one I'd found of me in a wig and ludicrous glasses at a
friend's fancy dress party. My confidence substantially fortified with wine, I decided that this, in fact, said all I needed to
say. 'No more Mr Nice Guy', I thought, and pressed save.

Looking at my now sparse and decidedly more edgy profile, I
raised a glass to my newly installed persona, shut down the
computer and went to bed.

The next day I headed out to work early so didn't get the chance to review the previous evening's reworking until the evening. During the day, I'd had a few moments of wondering if I'd been a bit rash to make those changes whilst I was a considerable amount of wine the wrong side of completely rational. I decided it would be easy to change it again later if I thought it looked rather less of an act of sheer brilliance viewed in the cold light of day than I had thought it to be the previous night. I doubted that many people would have seen it yet anyway, so put it out of my mind. When I finally made it home and checked my mail I was in for a big surprise. Overnight, no less than eight new messages had arrived along with a handful of 'winks'.

I was absolutely blown away.

For a moment I just stared while it sank in and was very glad I hadn't actually seen all this first thing that morning as I would undoubtedly have been very late for work. I sat down at my kitchen table and started reading through the various messages. Some were short and sweet, along the lines of 'Hey you, loving the sexy glasses', others were more involved and gave the impression of being really quite keen to meet up. I linked in to each profile in turn to see what the deal was with these people who'd suddenly all responded to my raunched-up new image having ignored my old one all this time. Gratifyingly, one of the messages and one of the winks were from people I'd previously messaged and who hadn't responded. My ego half thought 'pah, I'm not responding to you either, then' but I knew I wouldn't be able to resist replying eventually. What a difference a day makes. Suddenly, I'd gone from being stranded in the desert to finding the oasis and it felt fantastic.

Long Tall Ali

I replied to several of my new messages, but not all of them, having decided that one or two looked a little bit unappealing for one reason or another. The first one to come back to me was a single woman who appeared to be in her early thirties and who was very specific about her desire for one off encounters only. Her profile didn't give loads of information but there was a hint that she was quite tall so I was intrigued to see just how tall she might be, although, given my initial meet experience, it did cross my mind to wonder whether there was anything else she wasn't telling me. Keen to learn from past mistakes and put the experience to good use, I arranged an initial meet with Ali in a discreet location, very much of a mind to walk away immediately if I found myself in a similarly uncomfortable situation to the one I'd experienced with Miss M. Happily, I had no such reactions to this one. She certainly hadn't been kidding about her height, matching my six foot one frame and being slightly more heavily built to boot, but she carried it well and it looked great on her. I found her strikingly attractive.

We'd arranged to meet at a pleasant country-style pub on the outskirts of Winchester where we had a very civilised coffee and chatted for about forty minutes. Obviously very intelligent and highly educated, it seemed Ali also held a well-paid consultancy job in the technology industry. She was extremely interesting to talk to and became actively flirtatious as time went on. I genuinely liked her a lot. Having finished our coffee but still in the full flow of conversation we agreed to hang out a little longer and grab a bite to eat as it was now well into lunchtime.

49

Lunch rolled on into mid-afternoon and eventually she suggested we head back to her place for a little fun session. That
was more than okay with me as we'd built up a real rapport
by this time and I must admit my mind had been increasingly
wandering to visions of a physical encounter with her from
the moment we met. I'd have been quite disappointed to be
sent home at this stage. I followed her back to her place, an
unremarkable but spacious and comfortable apartment in a
period building. Our minds were obviously of one accord as,
still chatting away, we both automatically began undressing,
completely without hesitation or self-consciousness.

Naked, Ali's curves looked very fit and toned, an impressive,
very sexy physique. I was starting to tingle with the anticipation of getting my hands on her, and her hands on me! Our
conversation over the previous hour or so had left no doubts
about what we both wanted so now that we were alone there
was no reason to hold back. She seemed keen to get a taste
of me first and I was more than happy to lie back on the sofa
and let her have her way. She was very good too, almost deep
throating me in the process. Reclined in this sanctuary with
an attractive woman attached by the mouth to my nether
regions, I felt like an intrepid ocean explorer, sighting land
for the first time after many months at sea.

When she'd had a good long play I eased her away and got to
my feet, hauling her up to stand, legs wide, facing the end of
her sofa. Standing behind her, I savoured the sight of those
impressive curves before bending her forward and ramming
into her as she inhaled sharply, pushing back hard against
me. She was clearly ready for me, wet and inviting, immediately instigating a deep and rapid pace, her movements
strong and rhythmic, sometimes twisting and grinding,
moaning her pleasure all the while. It was perfect. She
seemed totally absorbed in it, shifting positions and calling
the shots while I simply went along with it and did my best
to comply, the advantage of this being that I was at liberty to

enjoy every aspect of the situation for its own sake. She didn't need me to give her anything but sex, a commodity I was happy to dish up in any quantity required. I ended up straddling her while she lay face down on the sofa, thrashing about like a woman possessed as she came. I let her ride the last waves before withdrawing and turning her over to unload over her fabulously large, firm breasts.

It wasn't, perhaps, the longest sex session I'd ever had but it had been a real joy getting acquainted with Ali. Perhaps knowing that sex with her was going to be a one-time-only event made it that little bit more intense too, no second tries here and no pressure to be building any future relationship either. I relished every moment, letting it sweep my mind clear of built-up frustrations, eventually leaving her apartment in a state of near euphoria.

Meeting Ali was a fantastic experience, completely changing how I felt about swinging. She was the proof I'd needed to convince myself that my hopeful plan could become reality, that there were sane, intelligent women whose company I could enjoy mentally and physically without emotional demands being made. I was so grateful to her for that. She was just a fabulous woman who, for whatever reasons of her own, wanted just what I wanted. It seemed logical to assume, then, that there were more like her out there and that this way of tackling my issues was actually going to be viable. It was the first time in three months of investigating this scene that I was completely convinced it could work for me. I was ecstatic.

I never really got to find out why she just wanted one-offs, didn't like to quiz her too hard about it in case I gave her the impression I wanted something more. Perhaps that was just her 'thing'. It did cross my mind that she might be in a relationship and just wanted occasional variety, although I didn't notice anything in her apartment to suggest that she was with anyone. I did message her afterwards, to thank her, and suggested it would be nice to keep in touch, perhaps even meet up every now and then if she wanted to, but I suppose if she'd wanted that then she'd have said so or messaged me back. In the absence of that I just had to respect her wishes and move on, albeit with renewed excitement and vigour.

The game had finally begun in earnest.

Gina Genie

As if I was now somehow being rewarded for my initial persistence in the face of adversity, my next encounter continued the upward trend. Gina, a single girl from Horsham, certainly had a great deal of photographic appeal and I was looking forward to meeting her with considerably more optimism than I'd dared to allow myself with earlier encounters. I had, however, still practiced a degree of caution and we had exchanged quite a few messages before agreeing to meet in The Angel Hotel in Midhurst one Saturday afternoon in late April. It was an unseasonably hot, sunny day and the slim, sweetly attractive and unnervingly innocent-looking Gina had, rather bravely I thought, turned up in a nice, silky dress. I admit I was envisioning removing it within minutes of meeting her. It looked like it would peel off oh-so-very-easily if I was only given the opportunity to get my hands on it.

For some reason, I'd been feeling a little self-conscious at the thought of meeting Gina, perhaps because she was rather younger than me, but I shouldn't have worried, we found plenty to chat about and it was an easy hour we spent together as we sipped our way through our coffees. I took to her very quickly, feeling almost instantly relaxed in her company. She told me she'd been swinging for quite a while but didn't do it intensively, using it to fill her spare time when she wasn't in a relationship and to add interest when she was in one, simply because she felt a need for variety and it suited her purpose. Although she confessed to having a couple of contacts whom she'd seen more than once she said this was rare as the point for her was mainly the frisson of the one off encounter.

David B

She was sounding more perfect by the minute.

We hadn't discussed in advance whether or not the meet might lead straight on to play. Still in the infant stages of exploring the etiquette of all this and not wanting to seem pushy, I'd left it open and didn't know if she had any plans or if she would even be prepared to take our first meet straight on to the next stage. However, the soft fabric grazing her thighs kept relentlessly drawing my attention to what lay beneath and I reminded myself that I, in reality, had nothing much to lose. Coffee cups sitting idle and empty, I suggested that it might be nice to continue our conversation back at my place, perhaps over a glass of wine in the garden where we could sit and enjoy the remains of the unexpectedly glorious afternoon sun. On balance, I was expecting her to decline, to be honest, as we hadn't covered the possibility of this occurring and I had no idea what she thought of me. She seemed perfectly happy to take up my offer, though, accepting with barely a flicker of surprise showing on her face, which I found quite beguiling and which allowed me to hope that she wasn't messing around and was (oh please, be true) actually just in this for the sex too. So we headed out to our cars and she followed me back home, with me alternating between speeding along at a pace, wanting to get her home as fast as possible, then slowing right down, suddenly concerned that she would fail to keep up and I might lose her.

Once there, I hurriedly made the formal introductions between Gina and the effusively welcoming Milton, grabbed a chilled bottle of Pinot from the fridge on my way past and, asking her to pick up a couple of glasses, ushered her straight through to the garden. The garden was looking brilliantly colourful and welcoming as we made our way down to the far end to sit on my antique white swing seat. A slightly poignant place for me as it held memories of my last moments with Lynn, but, with a little nod to my darling wife's memory, I determinedly pulled a curtain over that part of my mind and turned my attention back to Gina. We sat side by side, rocking gently in the sunshine, lulled into a pleasantly drifty state by the rhythm of the swing and the effects of the wine. We chatted idly, hints of flirtation creeping in, mostly, I admit, instigated by Gina. Looking back, she must have thought I was being incredibly slow but, novice as I was, I didn't want to make assumptions too early and scare her off. I began to make some more inquisitively provocative comments and quickly got the impression she was perfectly happy, impatient even, to take things further. Deciding to go for double or quits, I leaned in and kissed her neck. I was half waiting for her to jump up and run screaming from the garden but instead I got a welcoming sigh in response that had me tracing my way down with lips and tongue towards the neckline of that alluring dress. Glancing up briefly as I went, I saw that she'd let her head drop back, eyes closed, the hint of a smile on her lips. Relieved that the signs all looked good, I relaxed and carried on southwards.

Over the previous half hour or so, I'd been idly aware of the sounds in the background beyond the hedge, voices of the couple pottering in the next door garden while their young kids ran about playing some rumbustious game. There's a pretty thick hedge between the gardens though and the children's noise masked our low conversation so I felt pretty safe suggesting we get down to it right where we were. She yielded willingly to that idea and the sundress was soon up and over her head, proving my theory of easy removal, and I was taking in the view of her elfin-like, semi-naked body, with its pert little breasts, reclining provocatively on the swing. I was mesmerised by her delightfully tiny but so beautifully female frame. Hands and lips grazing her pale, alabaster-perfect skin, I travelled the length of her petite torso, electrified by her silky softness and by her seemingly hungry response to my attention. I felt fireworks going off in my brain as I explored delicately scented hair, fine cheekbones, delicate shoulders, petitely perfect breasts, taut belly, narrow thighs. All utterly divine.

Gradually the rocking of the swing became more vigorous as nature took its course and I was reluctantly forced to mentally leave my new-found paradise for a few moments as, at times, it was proving tricky to get good purchase on an undulating swing, more so than I'd anticipated, but I dug my toes in and pressed on as best I could. Gina and I occasionally smirked in acknowledgment at our joint attempts to keep our sounds low given the closeness of our still-oblivious neighbours, comfortably going about their mundane activities. Losing myself in the heavenly sensations of hands over flesh, lips on nipples, my shaft moving rhythmically inside her, reality was pushed further and further aside by the joyous liberation of pure sexual pleasure. Gina seemed lost too, face relaxed and distant, reclined across the slats at an angle that had allowed me to resolve my initial difficulties with the wayward swinging of the seat. And so we continued, contentedly rocking and fucking in the open sunshine, for quite some time before the first pricks of urgency began to kick in and the pace correspondingly increased. I shifted around slightly in a bid to accommodate the extra momentum without losing my grip on the ground and at the back of my mind I was vaguely wondering how this position was going to hold up as things really got going, though I can't say I was giving it much thought really being far too absorbed in the consuming delight of those moments swinging around with Gina.

Moments later, a small thud sounded on the ground beside us which instantly burst our secluded little bubble and brought us reeling back to reality, adrenaline kicking as we both turned and stared in horror at the miniature football rolling on the ground barely ten feet away from where we lay precariously balanced, more-or-less naked on the swing. Raised children's voices and an avid rustling in the hedge behind us cut through the last of the haze and we were then faced with the awkward business of urgent extrication mid-flagrante. My sense of not wanting to rip myself painfully out of her competed with the overwhelming and imperative desire not be observed in this position by a couple of kids who would doubtless be traumatised by the scene and likely never be able to look a football in the eye again as a result. Not to mention what the parents would have to say about it. Headlines flashed before my eyes.

Easing myself away as best I could I launched in ungainly fashion towards the ball, scooping it up and flipping it back over the hedge in one swift movement, rewarded with an instant ceasing of the juvenile attempt to break through the hedge and a cheerily innocent cry of 'thank you Mister' before the children's game resumed. I sank back onto the bench, head in hands, as we sat, side by side, in shock for a moment before, with an enquiring nod of my head, I suggested we head back to the house. She grinned and nodded then got to her feet, slipping the dress back on over her head whilst I scooped up clothes, wine and glasses. Shock already subsiding into amusement, we headed back up the path, hopelessly trying to suppress our snorts and giggles, to resume our own games indoors.

The adrenaline seemed to have fired us both up a bit and things had a more urgent edge from then on. I'd had enough of the seat-balancing act so led her past the sofa and on up to my room where we could romp in a rather less restrictive play area without danger of further interruption. Placing the wine glasses down, I turned her to face me, grabbed soft handfuls of her skirt and lifted the dress back up over her head in one easy movement, happily noting that I'd got my wish to remove it not just once but twice over. Underwear fully off this time too, before I got her to lean over, hands on the bed, while I hurriedly tore off my own clothes and set to work on her from behind, hands cupping and squeezing the gorgeous arse undulating before me, which I'd not yet had the opportunity to fully admire and which, rather erotically, still bore the slat marks from our swing session. She seemed to get straight back in the zone and she thrust herself back at me while I ran my hands up over her tiny waist to her breasts and really got stuck in, revelling in the opportunity to get good open friction on my whole length after the previous limitations.

Without withdrawing I shifted her forward on to the bed on all fours and continued ramming away but now with an extra view of it all in my bedroom mirror which just happens, by happy accident rather than by design, to be well placed for observing from this angle. She noticed it too and I could feel her body respond as the visual input evidently pleased her. She rose up on her knees and leaned back against me, arms in the air, giving me a spectacular view of her cute, beautifully shaped breasts, bouncing in unison in time with our energetic rhythm, my hands on her hips now, pulling her onto me as hard as I could. I'd started to feel the tingle building and when she reached between her legs and began to stroke me I had to bend her forwards, fighting to keep control and in danger of letting fly before she'd had enough.

She grabbed my hand and slid it between her thighs. Juices everywhere. I let my fingers slip back and forth, before focusing on her engorged clit, teasing it intensely with my fingertips. She dropped forward on the bed, trapping my hand and writhing against it, her body stiffening as her climax swiftly approached and built, then arching hard as it broke over her, leaving her bucking and squirming beneath me. Oh blessed release! I was now free to allow all those overwhelming sensations to break through, catapulting me on to my own release before she'd even finished hers. I stayed put until I was sure she was done then rolled exhaustedly away to lie next to her on the bed. She didn't move for quite a while and, though she'd given me no reason to think so, I was briefly concerned I might have broken her, tiny thing that she was. It was just an idle thought but when she continued to lie there, perfectly still, face down in my pillows, that seed of doubt began to grow.

'Gina?' I said, tentatively, suddenly terrified by the 'what-ifs'.

Nothing. I waited a few more seconds then tried again. Still no response. Anxious now I reached across, stroking her shoulder, then gently shaking it, then more firmly but to no avail. As I was preparing to get my arms underneath her to turn her over, slowly, to my immense relief, she shifted on to her side, exposing one mischievous chocolate-brown eye.

'Ye-eee-ssss?' she replied, stretching her face wide with a grin before breaking into giggles.

Grinning back with sheer relief, I leaned across and grabbed her playfully, tickling her sides in mock punishment until she was squeaking with laughter. Little minx.

Leaning back on the pillows, composure regained, we continued to chat for a little while before she decided it was time she headed off home. Unlike Ali, Gina had been perfectly forthcoming about her reasons for wanting one-off encounters but I couldn't let her leave without being clear about how much I'd enjoyed our time together and giving her the option to get in touch if she ever felt she wanted to. To date, she has not done so, which I can only assume, at this stage, means that I won't be hearing from her again, but that's the way of things in the wonderful world of swinging, everyone's in it for different reasons. It's very liberating being able to pick and choose your playdates knowing there's no obligation afterwards and for me that had solved at least part of the problem of my emotional disability almost overnight. I was overwhelmingly grateful to Gina for this second round of proof that swinging had good things to offer me as well as

David B

for the thoroughly enjoyable, highly entertaining and wholly satisfying afternoon we'd spent together.

Sometimes when life shuts a door really hard in your face you have no option but to eventually try to climb out of a window, even if the only window available seems like a pretty unfeasible means of escape.

Cracklin' Caroline

Having now spent a good deal of time on the only website I'd signed up with, I'd begun to feel a bit limited by the lack of new profiles available to check out. So I started investigating some of the many other similar websites and went on to sign up for a few, deciding it could potentially broaden the scope a bit even given the issue with verifications. Checking through a couple of these new sites for the first time, I spotted Caroline.

Caroline was a single mother of around forty, with a daughter in her late teens. I'd sent her a message but, given my previous experience of starting out with a brand new profile, I wasn't really expecting to get a reply. I was pleasantly surprised, then, when I did hear back from her after a day or two although it was a fairly short message. I immediately sent her a link to my main profile on the other site so that she had the option to have a look at my verifications and check that I was genuine. Apparently, she did go and have a look but even so it still took a couple of weeks of messaging before she felt confident enough to arrange a meet. I asked her if she would like to come to my house but her reply seemed hesitant so I suggested that perhaps we could meet in a pub not far from me for a drink and she could decide from there where she wanted to take things. She seemed much happier with that plan and we agreed to meet the following Sunday afternoon. It was a bank holiday weekend and I knew that neither of us would be working on the Monday so I mentioned that there was a bed available for her at the house, either mine or the one in the spare room, if she wanted to stay over but that she didn't need to make a decision about it in advance. Learning from my ambiguity with Ali and Gina, I thought I'd try to cover things before the event so we both knew what the options were.

I arrived at the pub around twenty minutes before our meet time to find a table with an open view of the door so I could keep an eye out for her arrival. I'd seen photographs so I recognised her when she appeared, but I think I'd have spotted her anyway as she positively slunk into the already busy pub, obviously jittery, scanning the tables anxiously until she'd spotted me and I had nodded an acknowledgement. As she made her way towards me I could see that she was slightly curvier in the hip department than I'd anticipated but had a really pretty face with rather beautiful green eyes and long, light hair. Altogether, a very attractive package.

I'd taken the liberty of ordering a bottle of wine and two glasses as it had come up in our online conversation that we both drank white. I poured her a glass as she was approaching and she sank into her chair with it gratefully attached to her lips before her bum had even made contact with the seat. She had downed that and was onto the next in less than ten minutes but it did the trick and in the interim she became visibly much more relaxed. I guess most of us are familiar to some degree with that irrational but awkwardly self-conscious feeling, that creeping suspicion which makes you think that everyone knows or suspects what you have done or are up to. It's a horrible sensation to experience but quite an amusing one to watch sometimes and Caroline had exhibited it to perfection. Fortunately, she appeared to lose that sensation once she'd made a good start on the wine. My expectations of further progress were fairly low having seen how nervous she had been but we settled into a nice, good humoured conversation and I found her very easy company. We were soon nattering away animatedly, our conversation conveniently masked by the background noise of the pub. This allowed us to begin to touch on some of the rather more delicate topics without too much fear of being overheard and, in fact, contrary to my expectations, it was she who suggested we head back to the cottage as we made our way towards the last dregs of the bottle. That was a very pleasant and welcome surprise.

This particular pub, though not my local, wasn't far from where I lived and as it was a nice day I'd decided to walk there from home. This meant I was able to get into her car to travel the short distance back with her, which I hoped would keep any remaining anxiety at bay, there being no directions to give, following to do or potential for getting lost. It all felt very normal and inconspicuous. She'd loosened up completely by this time and I had no desire for her to get the jitters again. I needn't have worried. She was raring to go, it seemed. I opened another bottle and poured her a glass, just to be sure. We'd chatted our way through barely half of that before she started being very flirty, to the point of asking me to get the old trouser snake out and let her have a look! By this stage he was quite excited about the prospect of putting on a show so I slowly released him and he poked his head out, enthusiastically, to take a look around. It wasn't long before he had a new admirer lavishing his favourite kind of attention on him and I sat happily back and let her pet him to her heart's content.

She was ardent and thorough in her attention too, having a tantalising technique of sucking me in then letting me slide out of her mouth almost all the way before slowly sucking me back in again, virtually full length. She went on with this, in and out, in and out, until I felt almost hypnotised watching her, the rhythmic anticipation gradually producing prickling sensations up and down my back. It was a mind-blowing feeling. She kept this up until I came, almost fully interred, at the back her throat. Suffice to say I was pretty impressed and, once recovered, made sure to tell her so.

We sat back on the sofa, working our way through most of the remains of the bottle before heading upstairs where I endeavoured to give her as much attention as she'd so benevolently given me, my tongue echoing her earlier technique to some degree whilst I drank in the taste of her, revelling once again in that rapturous sense of liberation before climbing aboard for what would prove to be a surprisingly lengthy session. She clearly just loved sex and would take as much as I could give her in any and every position we could think of. We must have used every square inch of the bed and room, sometimes in ways I hadn't even considered before, such as with her cantilevered, bridge style, hands on the dresser, feet on the bed while I stood between her legs, finding her positioned at the perfect height for some satisfyingly deep probing. She used the bedframe, the wardrobe, the door... It was enlightening and, occasionally, amusing, though I had to stop her climbing on the windowsill in pursuit of some other contortion she'd thought of. Whilst I'm not directly overlooked, I'd have had some explaining to do if I had been seen in compromising positions at my bedroom window by my friendly but ever-watchful neighbours. Just as I had started to wonder if she was ever going to want to stop, she came, suddenly and quite violently. It took me slightly by surprise and I had to gather myself together and complete the mission pretty quickly, suspecting she'd probably not be wanting too much more after the pounding she'd already taken. She snuggled up to me afterwards, virtually purring with contentment and full of smiles as we lay there, chatting and sipping wine for a while, before hunger overcame us and we headed down to the kitchen for snacks.

Apparently, Caroline had not been completely sated by our first instalment. Once recovered, fed and refreshed, she was almost immediately ready for another session, although, thankfully, not quite such an epic or energetic one the second time. She reclined, languorous and submissive, on the sofa while I rocked her fairly gently in contrast our earlier frenetic workout. Equally enjoyable in its way: no pressure, no gymnastics, just more glorious sex with a lovely, willing, contented woman. It was pretty blissful actually. She then stayed the night with me in my bed, waking me at about five a.m., clearly keen for yet more. A wonderfully insatiable woman, she just seemed to have no quantity limits at all. Caroline is one of the few women I've had ongoing meets with. No strings and no demands on either side, just a really fun fuck buddy. We get on extremely well both in and out of bed, making her a perfect partner for these kinds of interludes.

It's interesting, perhaps it might even seem slightly strange, to have repeated physical encounters with someone who you like, find attractive, respect and enjoy talking to without a relationship, in the full sense, developing. It was something I almost had a sense of 'watching' myself do, unsure as to how my emotions would deal with it and, frankly, ready to run like a jack rabbit if I started feeling a sense of Caroline's reliance on me emotionally. Thankfully, that didn't happen at all, it all stayed very light-hearted, undemanding and, above all, fun.

Sweet, sweet Caroline, if only there were more like you.

David B

Just A Private Dancer

The next meet I set up was with a couple. It was the first couple I'd opted to engage with since my very first full encounter but I was hopeful that this one might play out rather differently to that first session. I arranged to get together with Orla and her husband, Ben, after exchanging relatively few messages, at the French Horn pub in Alton on a Wednesday evening for an initial drink and chat. I hadn't seen many photos so I was surprised and incredibly pleased when I finally met them. They were a tall, good-looking duo, but, more importantly, they immediately seemed like my kind of people. Mahogany-haired and potently attractive, Orla was definitely dressed to impress in a gorgeous, cleavage-enhancing, short black dress, which barely concealed the tops of her stockings. Naturally enough, that caught my attention straight away. They were open and friendly and the meet went very well, although the rapidly progressing flirtatiousness of our conversation was slightly inhibited by the quiet atmosphere of the pub that night. There was an instant affinity between the three of us, though, an immediate easy banter, increasingly with suggestive undertones, and much laughter. The twinkly, exuberant Orla definitely seemed up for a fun time and I was really looking forward to spending some time with them. We parted company after having a great evening, unanimously and enthusiastically agreeing to get together again the following week.

They arrived at my house fairly late on Friday evening, probably around nine thirty. This was at their request and had surprised me a little but it wasn't a problem. I greeted them at the door and instantly felt it had been worth the wait as I was visually knocked out by the sight of a smiling Orla, illuminated in the porch light, wearing an incredibly clingy and alluringly short red dress. I could see beneath her long, loose jacket that the dress was cut away at the sides, showing off her tiny waist and curvy hips, plunging at the front to show off her magnificent, page-three-worthy cleavage. With stunning legs on show too, she was, physically, damned near perfect. She exuded sexual confidence, positively glowed with it, leaving me almost speechless. I couldn't take my eyes off her.

Drinks in hand, we immediately picked up where we'd left off previously, laughing and joking flirtatiously as we relaxed on the sofa. I wasn't sure how this meet was going to play out and was about to suggest a quick trip to the hot tub to get things started when Orla suddenly threw a furtive look at Ben, got up and disappeared back outside with a sly wink saying she needed to get something from the car. I was instantly intrigued, my radar switched up, wondering what was going to happen next. She arrived back in the room a minute or two later with a large black bag and a small holdall. I was even more intrigued as she produced from the bag a mobile, adjustable pole, leaving it with Ben to put into position while she went upstairs with the holdall.

She reappeared, once Ben had finished setting up, having changed into a microscopically cheeky police uniform complete with hat and truncheon.

Previously, whilst we'd been chatting, I'd been playing tracks from my vinyl collection and Orla had flicked through a few covers, pulling some out and presenting them to me with a request to play some specific tracks. So I set them up, started the first track and then sat back on the sofa with Ben to watch her as she performed for us. My sweet, long-suffering Milton had been quite enthusiastic in his greeting when Ben and Orla had arrived, leading me to have high hopes for the evening. He now sat rigidly to attention at the side of the sofa, watching intently as she writhed and slithered around her pole. This puzzled me initially, as he seemed to be watching her routine with an almost human intensity of appreciation, which I wouldn't have expected of him. It wasn't until she let the truncheon fall to the ground and it rolled away that the real focus of his absorption became apparent. Unluckily for Milton, a nice game of Fetch was not on the agenda for that night. Sadly for me, as I was yet to find out, Bury the Bone was not going to be on the games menu either. Only once she had finished treating us to her erotic display, did it become apparent that Orla was an 'exhibitionist', i.e. someone who is happy to put on a show but not to physically interact, so I only got to watch and not to touch, something I wasn't made aware of until that night. As for the performance itself, well, what can I say? She certainly knew how to work her audience and it was an incredibly sexy routine. Within fifteen minutes or so she had stripped completely naked, twisting and grinding on that pole before working herself down it to the ground, where she proceeded to give us some very nice views while playing with herself until she started to shudder and came all over my nice wooden floor! Absolutely fabulous to watch, of course, although it wasn't quite how I'd expected the evening to go.

Looking back on it, they really should have declared their intentions before coming round and I think a different person might have been rather less tolerant of being left stranded after a show like that. It would be pointless to get too wound up about these things though, I guess. Truth be told, it was a unique and very pleasurable experience, regardless of the lack of physical interaction. After all, how many people can say they've had a private pole show, for free, by a seriously hot, naked woman in their own sitting room? So I'm not complaining, not at all, though I think I can be forgiven for knocking one out after they'd packed up and gone home.

All in all a fantastically nice couple and a titillatingly fun, if slightly frustrating experience. Meeting in other circumstances, I think we might well have become good friends but, given that friendship wasn't what any of us were after and that, quite honestly, I am sexually wound up enough already without watching a stunning but untouchable woman gyrating around in front of me, I won't be seeing them again, since it really is the sex I'm in this for, after all.

David B

The Sound of the Not-So-Silent Ms S

As I have mentioned, I live in a quiet rural village. My house sits in a small terrace of cottages in a cul-de-sac, is not really overlooked and, aside from my immediate neighbours has no passing traffic, making it relatively easy to keep my encounters discreet and private. For quite some time, despite the close call in the garden with the neighbours' children, this idyllic situation had kept my lifestyle well below anyone's notice, but the problem with living in a small village is that it doesn't take much to register a blip on the community radar and once there's a hint of a scent, they're off after it like a pack of blasted bloodhounds. So, I was cautious and careful but, after a period with not so much as the twitch of a neighbourly curtain, I started to relax, thinking I had the situation pretty well under control. Everything was in a nice, stable holding pattern until along came Ms S.

Ms S was one of the few ladies, certainly in the early days, whom I invited home without a prior meet. We'd had some fairly lengthy chats online, I'd seen quite a few photos, her profile seemed very genuine, with some good verifications, and she was enticingly keen to get started. It just felt, on balance, like it was all going to be fine. Also, in my defence, it was another one of those beautiful, sunny, early summer days, when the world seems a heavenly, happy place and everything has that sense of having relaxed down almost into slow motion. Peaceful and perfect. This ambience lured me into letting my guard down just a little; after all, what could be more pleasant than spending an afternoon exploring the uncharted waters of a newly discovered ocean of potential? What could possibly go wrong?

I knew that Ms S was slightly older than me but I had seen a
good selection of pictures and she appeared to have a rather
nice body, sporting a remarkably fine example of the ample,
rounded bosom that I favour. If I'm honest, this was possibly an additional factor in my decision to invite her straight
over as, I confess, there is little more enticing to me than the
female breast. The more voluptuous the better but I love
them all, every last bouncing, bobbling one of them. She did
not disappoint either, I could instantly tell I was going to
enjoy those, in fact the heat of the day was rapidly translating
to another kind of heat that had me increasingly fixated on
those beautiful breasts from the moment she arrived. Grabbing the customary bottle of wine, we headed down to the
far end of the garden where we rocked gently on the swing
seat, sipping and chatting and, eventually, kissing and groping. Oh those breasts! I felt an overwhelmingly urgent desire
to release them from their captivity and immerse myself in
their abundant pink glory. Although the balmy weather made
an alfresco encounter quite appealing, the still-too-recent
memory of my narrow escape from neighbourly discovery,
coupled with the evident sounds of garden occupants on all
sides, made me think better of it.

Without stopping to explain my reasons, I led Ms S, wine still
in hand, inside and upstairs to my bedroom. Her close-fitting
top appeared to be straining at the seams so I lost no time in
removing it before slowly and deliberately unhitching her bra
and releasing those luscious mammarian mountains. Kneeling at the edge of my bed, as she lay propped up on her elbows, I marvelled at those twin miracles of female engineer-
ing for a while, cradling and stroking each in turn whilst my
tongue traced their nipples and outlines. They were unbeliev-
able. Unable to contain myself any longer, I buried my face
between their consuming expanses, enraptured and ecstatic.

Miss S was showing signs of becoming pretty excited herself
so I took a moment to remove the rest of her clothes, along

with my own, before taking equal pleasure in indulging her lower regions too, running my tongue gently over her clit and teasing it back and forth before pushing my tongue deep into her. She cried out and I felt her body tense, knees lifting slightly, her hands in my hair, pulling me harder on to her. She was mumbling something but I couldn't quite make out what, though it seemed positive and she looked like she was enjoying herself. Her pawing hands seemed to need something to do though, so suddenly inspired, I turned half circle and straddled her, knees above her shoulders, dropping my cock into her mouth whilst I continued to probe her with my tongue. She responded very enthusiastically to this change of position and we spent a long, mutually intense time in our two-way pleasuredome. Eventually, it became evident that she was getting extremely keen to have me inside her. I knew this because she lost no opportunity to tell me, gaspingly, all about it, loudly enough for me to hear despite having my ears firmly wedged against her thighs. But even this level of verbal enthusiasm didn't prepare me what was to come next. Relenting to her increasingly insistent encouragement, I turned and lowered myself until I was suspended over her, teasing her gently with the tip of my cock until she loudly pleaded, virtually demanded, for me to get on with it and I obligingly eased inside.

It was immediately apparent that this excited Ms S very much indeed. Before I'd even had time to turn my attention back to her pendulous top half she had started bucking and arching beneath me then, out of the blue, yelled "FUCK ME, DAVE! FUCK ME HARD…OHH, OOOHHH....I MEAN IT, FUCK ME AS HARD AS YOU CAN... OHHHHH... OOOHHH… AGGHHHHH..."

Right. That would be 'S' for SCREAMER then!

Wow, I really mean she was properly screaming. I've never heard anything like it before or since. Oh my GOD!

I was unprepared for this aural onslaught and equally unprepared for the reaction it got from gentle, loyal Milton, patiently sitting downstairs awaiting our reappearance. Milton was definitely not happy about the screaming. Perhaps Milton thought I was being attacked. In any case, Milton began to howl, long, soulful, heartfelt howls of anguish from the foot of the stairs. Trying not to break my stride, since Ms S still appeared to be enjoying herself very much, and, granted, so was I, (although I was slightly concerned for my future hearing capability), I attempted to pacify Milton with such calming words as 'SHUT UP YOUR YOWLING, YOU NOISY MUTT!' and similarly encouraging phrases. I did my best to time these between Ms S's screeching and the dog's howls, no mean feat and almost certainly the closest I've ever come to successful multi-tasking. Milton, however, remained distressed and Ms S, who seemed totally unaware of any of the sounds emanating from either myself or from Milton, continued to squeal away happily.

I decided there was nothing for it but to push on through, as I still had a rather enjoyable rhythm going. So I just got on with the job, doing my best to block out the worst of the racket and having refrained from the option of buffering myself from some of the noise by covering Ms S's face with a pillow, a thought which had only momentarily crossed my mind as a possible solution.

At last, after an ear-shatteringly noisy orgasm from my gratifyingly enthusiastic lover, fully sated, we lay exhausted, side by side, chests heaving in tandem while we recovered. Still breathing heavily and very warm from the exertion, I glanced gratefully up towards the window through which a pleasant, cooling breeze was flowing. Seconds later, horror hit me like a brick as my mind processed the potential implications of this combination of circumstances. Muttering quiet pleas to a benevolent universe, I pushed up onto my elbows and surreptitiously scanned the neighbouring gardens. My heart sank as I made out the tops of no less than three of my neighbours' heads scattered within my range of view. It was plainly obvious from the angles of those heads that they were all rigidly fixated in the direction of my window, like a pride of hungry lions on the Serengeti who had, perchance, just noticed a lame gazelle in their midst, leaving me with the sure and certain knowledge that questions would be asked.

Fortunately, Ms S seemed blissfully oblivious to any of this and, deciding to spare her blushes, I made no mention of it. In due course I escorted her out to her car, and bid her farewell. All was peaceful, but I couldn't help noticing from the corner of my eye a tell-tale curtain twitch of the type I had striven so hard to avoid. Retreating hastily back indoors, I took refuge in the kitchen whilst I contemplated my options and attempted to console the bewildered Milton with a pat and a handful of biscuits. I eventually came to the conclusion that after several years in such a small community, most of my neighbours and I knew one another well enough for me to be upfront with them and just brazen it out. So that is what I did, with more than a little trepidation, but hopeful that they would be understanding of my predicament. I'm happy to say that those I confided in were indeed understanding. This acceptance of my unexpected change of lifestyle was probably helped by their knowledge of my history, having watched me suffer through Lynn's illness and witnessed my subsequent difficulty in coming to terms with her death.

I was deeply relieved and grateful for their support or, at least, lack of adverse reaction, not to mention their forgiveness regarding recent levels of local noise pollution. However, if I wasn't much mistaken, I definitely detected a distinct glimmer of titillation. Well, it is a very quiet area where not an awful lot goes on and I got the impression that they were really quite open to the prospect of the occasional erotic interlude occurring in the vicinity, if only for the entertainment value. I quietly made a mental note to keep a close eye on the window situation from here on in and perhaps increase the height of my hedges. Whilst I'm quite happy being watched in action by prior arrangement with all concerned, I was not thrilled at the prospect of providing a local alternative to the Nine O'clock News for those with a possible voyeuristic tendency.

In the immediate aftermath of my session with Ms S, I'd felt surprised, perhaps even slightly outraged, that none of the verifications on her profile had mentioned her verbal tendencies. Flattering as it might have been to think so, I didn't believe for a moment that her ardent vocals were something which had made their presence felt for the first time today. Why did nobody warn me? It wasn't until I sat down to write her a verification myself that I hesitated. After all, it had been unfortunate that circumstances had been as they were and had led to my secret life being discovered, but she hadn't actually done anything wrong. Thinking back, had it really been all that loud? It seemed a bit mean to say anything too specific so I just called it 'enthusiastic' and left it at that, in doing so, perfectly answering my own question.

David B

The Spy Who Bugged Me

I am acquainted with all of my neighbours, since it's a rather small and close-knit community, but am friendlier with some than with others. There was a bit of banter with those I knew best, knowing looks or nods of acknowledgement from some others, but without question word had clearly now got around about my activities. I was okay with that as their attitude had been so accommodating but responses did vary slightly. One of my immediate neighbours, Ned, with whom my garden shared a boundary, was one of those I knew slightly less well and who definitely fell into the 'knowing looks' camp. Something I detected in those looks made me pause for thought. What was it? A slight lewdness possibly? Whatever it was, it made me a tad wary and before too long, my wariness was proven to be justified.

Having decided to take another chance on the 'couples' option, I was being visited by what turned out to be a tremendously up-for-it pair, Mr & Mrs P, on a sunny summer afternoon. Mrs P was a good-time girl who became more and more raucous and less and less inhibited as the afternoon wore on and the wine went down. I suggested we make the most of the decent weather and decamp to the tub, which we did with much jocular merriment as, by this time, we were starting on our third bottle of wine. Soon we were comfortably ensconced, chatting and laughing and splashing about in the welcoming bubbles.

Ned's garden runs right alongside mine but I am not easily overlooked, although, of course, there is always the potential for a view over the hedge if you have a ladder or are prepared to climb a little. I hadn't really thought that my neighbours were voyeuristic enough to go so far as that so it hadn't troubled me at all. On that balmy and essentially windless afternoon, however, as I was enjoying the now familiar sensations of slippery wet naked bodies touching and sliding beneath the frothy surface, I gradually became aware of a suspicious kind of rustling from Ned's side of the hedge. I kept this to myself for a little while until I was pretty certain that my assessment of the situation was correct, then quietly made Mr & Mrs P aware of this development and we watched with giggling, slightly drunken interest to see what would happen next. Slowly but surely, the top of a familiar head came into view, followed tentatively by a pair of eyes which switched from slitty inquisitiveness to alarm as the suspicion dawned that he might have been spotted. The head retracted sharply but, after a brief respite, the rustling continued. Mrs P was finding the whole situation utterly hilarious and her ill-disguised snorts and giggles must have given that away but Ned was plainly on a mission and not to be deterred. Soon, the top of his head began to emerge from the shrubbery once again. Unable to contain herself any longer, the irrepressible Mrs P drew herself up out of the water ensuring that Ned was about to get the eyeful of a lifetime. She was a well-built lady with a gloriously impressive set of knockers of which she was unashamedly proud. She rose from the tub, water cascading down her body and trickling alluringly from her nipples, just as Ned made full eye contact. Giving an extravagant shimmy in his direction she then grabbed a couple of handfuls, pushing them up and together, and shouted out 'GET A LOAD OF THESE BEAUTIES MATE!'

Whilst Mr P and I absolutely fell about, snorting and hooting with laughter, the poor, ill-prepared Ned, after a moment of horrified rigor mortis, made a strange gargling sound and abruptly descended below the foliage, with a crash and 'ouch' rapidly followed by a rather pained 'fuck it'! I had to laugh when I witnessed him hobbling about a few days later and asked him in passing if he'd hurt himself. 'Gardening injury', came the somewhat sheepish reply, his eyes averted.

Unperturbed, by Ned's antics and, in fact, perhaps made bolder by our own (or at least Mrs P's) brazenness, we went on to enjoy a thoroughly entertaining time in the tub together that night, the balmy, starry evening boosting the sense of 'trenches spirit' and camaraderie in the face of uninvited invaders. Mrs P's breasts were wonderful, so full and voluptuous that Mr P and I drunkenly amused ourselves by taking it in turns to bury our faces in them, laughing our heads off as we tried to work out if we could wrap them all the way round to meet behind our heads. It's a shame you can't really have soap in a hot tub without a massive clear up operation being required the following day as I reckon she had the most perfect cleavage for a soapy-tit-wank, an opinion my inebriated mind saw fit to convey to Mr P who nodded enthusiastically and confirmed that my judgement was, in his experience, absolutely correct.

Hands were starting to wander further now too, and while Mr P had his between Mrs P's legs, she reached over and began playing with me. Already half hard from the situation, I responded quickly to her touch. Suddenly, she grabbed me by the dick and pulled me up to standing.

'Oh look, we've got ourselves a nice big catch here' she said to Mr P, turning me this way and that to get a good look before leaning forward and taking me straight into her mouth. 'I'm not sure you're going to get that down in one' said Mr P and we all fell about laughing once again. He was right though, she couldn't but she gave it a pretty good try before moving her attentions on to her patiently amiable husband.

While she was busy with her mouth full of Mr P, I reached out and stroked my hand up and down her back. Reaching behind, she pulled me towards her, arching her bum back so I was left in no doubt as to what she wanted. I moved in close behind her, slipping easily inside her in the ready wetness of the tub and we were underway. I was now in one of my favourite situations, engaged with a woman who was also occupied elsewhere leaving me to enjoy the moment at my leisure. I started moving rhythmically back and forth, mesmerised by the way her pillow breasts floated and swayed just below the water in time with our movements. I reached forward to fondle them, intrigued as always, at how being immersed in water seemed to completely change the feel and texture of them, watching, fascinated when they broke the surface now and then as she shifted position to get a better angle on her husband.

After a while, she rose up out of the water and perched herself on the side of the tub, leaning back slightly and looking enquiringly at the two of us.

'Go on then, Dave' said Mr P.

'You sure you don't want a go?' I said, politely.

'S'okay' he said, 'It's your tub.'

Despite the effect of copious quantities of alcohol, in my mind the obvious response of 'but it is your wife' presented itself. However, somehow catching the comment before it actually emerged, I managed to switch it for something along the lines of 'Well, thanks very much, that's most kind' and got stuck in.

It is possible to be too polite in these situations, as I had discovered before.

David B

Although the still-warm evening made it fairly comfortable being partly out of the water, I knew from experience that the position Mrs P had assumed just wasn't going to work long term. I'd already enjoyed the view from behind so, keeping her facing me, I knelt on the tub seat, drawing her off the side and attempting to hold her at a suitable level in the water for me to find my way in. Easier said than done, especially with a distracting face-full of pendulous mammaries to contend with, but I persevered and we had a short-ish interlude in that position before we conceded defeat and I switched places with her, angling myself so she could sit down on me easily. She was well away by now and I was treated to the resulting sensations of her enthusiastic bouncing on me twinned with the effects that her generous breasts created. In and out of the water they went, nipples cascading each time, the resultant mini tsunamis reverberating off the sides of the tub. My face became slightly overwhelmed with the increased splashing as she built up her pace, it was like watching a couple of playful baby elephants cavorting at the edge of a watering hole.

Mr P had been watching this develop with a benignly amused look on his face but as the splashing intensified he began to laugh out loud and we were all soon howling once again, Mrs P played to the crowd, twisting from side to side, sweeping her copious breasts in arcs across the water, sending showers everywhere. Helplessly convulsed with laughter, neither Mr P nor I had the slightest hope of retaliating. Eventually, feeling rather like I'd been water-boarded by an enthusiastically playful walrus, I suggested it might be an idea to go back inside for more play before one of us actually drowned, so we clambered out of the tub and ran, dripping, back to the house. After a slightly uncoordinated three way rub down and the pouring of fresh drinks, we had a final romp on the rug in the sitting room which ended with me eventually inducing an orgasm from the still-giggling Mrs P before withdrawing and preparing to unload over her voluptuous head-

80

lights. Unexpectedly, Mr P joined forces from the other side of her and we ended up having an almost simultaneous release in the same direction. It was another new experience to tick off the list, along with the sight of a woman smearing the juice of two freshly squeezed men over her body, but I was surprising myself with how rapidly I was becoming accustomed to accepting, even embracing, this kind of thing and she did look comely laying there, glistening with her new paint job. Some things were easier to get used to than others and I'd found this one a little challenging. No doubt I would have left Mr P to go it alone if I'd had less wine inside me, or if the general rowdiness of our evening hadn't loosened me up so much in advance.

The thing I'd struggled most with on this particular night had first struck me when I'd started playing with couples. Despite the boys-school, after-gym-showers experience which meant I'd seen, albeit completely obliviously, plenty of naked guys in my time, I realised I'd never been around another guy with a hard-on before. The first time I was in that situation I found it slightly disconcerting and a bit uncomfortable, although that had passed fairly quickly and, after a few times, it barely registered. I suppose you just have to adopt a 'get on with it' attitude unless it's something you absolutely can't deal with. The end game tonight had been the first time I'd been in close proximity with another guy who was not only hard but also actively masturbating right in front of me and it had certainly pushed back another boundary.

Mr & Mrs P left me at around midnight, slipping quietly off down the road to their waiting taxi after Mrs P had waved and whispered a final giggling, cheery goodbye in the direction of Ned's house, which had us all bent over once again trying to suppress our laughter. They were tremendously fun people and it had certainly been an entertaining night. I slept like a log after all that laughing and shagging.

David B

We kept in touch for some while afterwards, with the idea of getting together again, but it was just one of those things that never quite happened and after a few months I suppose we all just drifted away in our different directions and on to other things. They were a great couple, though, and our night together was not one I'll forget in a hurry.

Sisters, Sisters

My newfound openness with my neighbours sometimes became a source of amusement. Despite their acceptance of my extra-curricular activities, they were evidently uninitiated in the ways and possibilities of my current existence; but also, perhaps, rather intrigued, albeit sometimes in an almost disbelieving way. One or two of them would regularly ask me how I was and if I was 'playing' that week and I confess I took some pleasure in toying with the boundaries of their belief. Over time they acclimatised and eventually came to embrace the entertainment value of my encounters, sometimes co-ordinating their activities so they could watch my prospective partners as they arrived, even going so far as to give them marks out of ten if they were in a playful mood.

On one occasion, I happened to cross paths with a neighbour, Tony, with whom I'm on very friendly terms. We chatted briefly and he asked if I had any activities planned for that week. I replied that, yes, I was expecting company that very night and that it involved two sisters, slightly smirking to myself as his jaw hit the floor. 'Sisters! You lucky bugger!' were his words, as I recall.

I told him what time they were due to arrive and it was no surprise to glimpse his shadow lurking in his upstairs window as I walked the girls up to the house, having been waiting for them at the bottom of the road so they'd know where to park. It seemed that he must have forewarned a few of the other neighbours too as there seemed to be people at almost every window. Plainly eager to get a closer look, by the time we reached the top of the short incline up to the row of houses, Tony and another neighbour, Roger, emerged simultaneously, through their front doors and headed towards us, both obviously trying to look nonchalant but instead looking self-conscious and a bit awkward. I called out a cheery 'Hello' and waved, their sheepishly returned waves reflecting their slight embarrassment. I thought it was hugely funny and it did make it all the more entertaining when I was later recounting to them some elements of what turned out to be a truly amazing meet.

When I'd first seen Leigh and Jenna's profile, I'd been a bit suspicious as it looked like it could have been one of those fake ones which are supposed to lure you into ringing a sex line or have you buying things or signing up for some subscription or other. However, I did go in and take a look, pleased to find that they had quite a long list of very positive verifications. It appeared they had been on the swinging scene for quite some time and had a string of satisfied playmates in their wake to prove it.

I lost no time in getting in touch.

I had a response from Leigh the following day and she and I then went on to exchange a few friendly and informative emails, from which I discovered that she and her sister were in their thirties, Leigh the elder by a couple of years, that they lived together in Brighton, were unmarried (although Jenna had been married at one time) and that they enjoyed one another's physical company very much. However, they enjoyed it even more when there was a man around for them to play with too. They had found a solution to the slightly unusual nature of their preferences by using swinging websites and it suited them to perfection, offering them an endless list of playdates with free-spirited, non-judgemental partners and allowing them to live their chosen lifestyle within a community of like-minded souls, their situation accepted and generally heartily embraced. That really struck a chord with me as that was why I was here too.

And they were sisters.

What could be more perfect?

After we'd discussed the possibility of meeting up, Jenna, hitherto unseen, started to make an appearance in the emails, seeming similarly open and forthcoming, which was a relief as I'd been wondering why the communication was all from Leigh up to that point. It made perfect sense as soon as I met them but with no real knowledge of their relationship it had been a mild question mark over their validity for me. With Jenna now comfortably on board, however, and having seen so many positive verifications, I invited them to my house without a prior get together. On this occasion, fortunately, my instincts proved to be correct and we clicked instantly. After the rather obvious encounter with the bumbling duo of Tony and Roger on our way to the house, I did explain to them that my neighbours were aware of my circumstances and warned them that there was potential, at least from one quarter, of a spot of voyeurism. They were utterly unperturbed by this prospect. Experienced as they were, I think they would actually have relished the opportunity to perform for an audience but the hapless Ned did not put in an appearance for this session. He would have been in for quite a treat if he had though.

The girls were actually very attractive, both of them, with long hair, lovely figures and that air of sexual confidence which I find extremely galvanising. Whilst we'd been messaging, it had crossed my mind to wonder if they were genuinely sisters or just using that suggestion as a ruse to make them more appealing. Short of asking them for birth certificates or something similar as proof, there wasn't really any way of knowing, so it seemed pointless to ask. On first impressions, they certainly appeared similar enough to be convincing so I decided to leave it at that and just take it at face value.

They were casually dressed but that only enhanced the relaxed, carefree, ready-for-anything impression they were giving off. I warmed to them immediately, as did Milton, who gave them an ebullient welcome as I ushered them into the house. I led the way through towards the kitchen offering them wine as I went. Not hearing a response, I looked back and was greeted with the unexpected sight of the pair of them already in action. Leigh had Jenna pressed up against the wall, pinning her arms back above her head while kissing her deeply. I watched, transfixed, as they indulged themselves, an unexpected pleasure which became an increasingly intense experience for me as they seemed to lose themselves in their enjoyment of the moment and I was left tingling on the sidelines. Not surprisingly, this erotic show was having a profound effect on me. Spellbound, I was perfectly content, for a moment, to play watcher to their arousing performance. It was fascinating. Fairly quickly, though, I began to feel compelled to join in, it was just too enticing. Seeming to sense this, Leigh pulled back from Jenna, smiled at me and then said cheerily 'let's go grab that wine and hit the hot tub'. Excellent plan, I thought. I was starting to really like Leigh, she was so switched on, definitely a natural leader. Already, I would have done anything she asked or told me to do with a joyful heart and a smile on my face.

Naked, the super-sexy sisters did not disappoint in any way. It was all starting to seem a bit surreal. They were so interactive, so hypnotically gorgeous. No question that this was going to take a top slot on my list of all time memorable experiences. Time had slowed almost to a stop as we drifted outside to immerse ourselves in the gently bubbling water, sipping wine and enjoying the gathering sunset. Arms and legs gently bumping and grazing beneath the surface, almost innocently yet so charged I felt like my skin was on fire, then hands, softly touching, stroking, becoming bolder, bodies getting closer, skin gliding on skin, eventually becoming a writhing tangle of limbs and breasts and tongues. I felt as though I was in the hands of angels. They seemed to be telepathic, those heavenly girls. Without so much as a glance at one another, they simultaneously began to lift me out onto the side of the tub, allowing them to access the now throbbing eagerness I was struggling to contain. It took every ounce of self-control to hold back the inevitably threatening surge which I could feel rapidly building as they set to work in tandem, but I was utterly determined not to cut this experience short by a single second more than I could possibly hold out for.

Leigh, naturally, chose the perfect moment to move things indoors. She set the pace and scenarios throughout the whole session but did it in a way that made everything flow. It wasn't a cold night but sitting out on the side of the tub had been slightly chilly, despite the blazing inferno now burning between my legs. We climbed out and wrapped our arms around each other, grabbing towels and rubbing down as we worked our way back to the house and upstairs to the bedroom. Leigh suggested I film her and Jenna together for a while, another perfect move. It was so amazing watching them but filming made me focus even more, giving it a dual quality that enhanced the whole experience. Catching some film to look back on after the event, if only to prove to myself that this dream-like scenario had actually occurred, was also something I was very glad to have. Leigh, once again, masterminded the scenario, setting about pleasuring her sister, pausing every now and then, whenever Jenna appeared to be reaching a peak, and turning her attention to me while Jenna regained control. Eventually, Jenna's moans built to a crescendo and she had her noisy, shuddering release, on the tip of Leigh's tongue. It would have been all too easy for me to unload at that point, in fact it was only with superhuman restraint that I held it in, but, again, I emphatically did not want this session to end any time soon and that thought kept me back from the brink. Just.

Leaving Jenna to regain her composure for a moment, Leigh started looking in her bag for something while I put down my camera and topped up our glasses, watching with interest to see to see what Leigh would do next. Smiling tantalisingly at me, she placed down beside her a blindfold, two pairs of handcuffs and a 'Rampant Rabbit' vibrator. She made no comment about this array of paraphernalia, but it lay openly on the bed in full view. She kept full eye contact with me, still smiling, as I tried, unsuccessfully, not to let my gaze keep flicking over to the items she'd laid out, and she just chatted nonchalantly away, as if we were just sitting across a table in some café.

We sipped away at our wine and chatted until Jenna had reached the point where she could join in. A few more minutes and Leigh gently started working on Jenna once again. They obviously had a bit of a dominant/submissive thing going on between them, Leigh always the dominator, with more than a touch of exhibitionism thrown in. She started by gently stroking Jenna, long gentle caresses all over her until she lay back and closed her eyes, her body responding visibly to Leigh's touch. Leigh then tied the blindfold over Jenna's eyes, still, somehow, chatting away to me as she did so, the sounds staying the same but the undercurrent of mood suddenly changing as we all became aware that the games were about to begin again and a tingle of anticipation filled the already electrified air. I wondered if she was planning to handcuff me too but she used both sets on Jenna, splaying her arms against the bedframe before giving life to the Rabbit and starting to tease Jenna with it. I watched, fascinated, fresh waves of horny excitement breaking over me, my poor beleaguered chap rising fully again in an instant. Working on Jenna with increasing intensity, Leigh suddenly turned to me and said those three little words that every man longs to hear: 'fuck me...now'. I didn't need to be told twice.

I eased up behind the happily occupied Leigh, sliding my fingers through her juices before plunging in with vigour. Perhaps not surprisingly I was ready to fire off almost immediately which combined with the sounds I was hearing from Jenna, who was obviously on the brink again herself, made it a monumental exercise in self-control not to let go straight away. Mercifully, I didn't have long to wait though. As Jenna's noisy climax reverberated once more around the room, I felt Leigh's muscles start to contract, her hand reaching round to pull me harder into her. She was much more controlled than Jenna, gasping quietly as the waves hit her, then moaning softly as she felt me tip over the edge myself, thrusting deep and crying out with the sheer fucking relief of finally letting go after such a torturously long build up.

Through the subsequent fog, I think Leigh and I both became aware simultaneously of the buzzing and squealing from Jenna, who was still at the mercy of the relentless Rabbit vibrating away deep inside her, hands tied and helpless. Leigh switched it off and gently removed it while I eased back from her and knelt on the bed feeling utterly exhilarated. What a session. What a fucking amazing session! I was already blown away by what had gone on that evening but, as it turned out, it still wasn't over. I was just kneeling there, basking in the perfection and satisfaction of it all, when Leigh spotted that I was still quite erect. A flash of surprise crossed her face and she looked enquiringly at me. I explained that he rarely seemed to quite go limp after the first time and her surprise turned to a smile when she realised there was more action to be had.

'I want you to cum over Jenna'" she said.

Well, I was hardly likely to argue with a request like that...

I got the impression this was not the first time they'd played out this scene as, once again they seemed to act in perfect unison. Released from her cuffs and blindfold, Jenna laid back on the pillows, running her hands languidly over herself and what she could reach of me while Leigh licked and sucked me fully back to life. The visual impact, coupled with Leigh's expert work had me hurtling back towards the brink very quickly. Feeling me starting to quiver, Leigh guided me over to Jenna's mouth where I released a fresh load coating her lips and chin. As I knelt there, almost numb with pleasure, Leigh leaned down and kissed Jenna, sharing the contents of her mouth and licking the spillage off her chin before turning back to me, opening her mouth and rolling the contents round her tongue before swallowing with a smile. Dear God! My mind was turning circles on itself by this point and all I could do was watch them, lost in a state of awestruck wonder.

As high points go, that whole experience was right up there at the top of the memory-bank 'special events' file. Certainly, the vision of two gorgeous women licking my manly residues off one another is not a sight that I ever thought I would see!

Reeling now from the intensity, I sank onto the bed and we all continued to just sprawl there, still naked, for about half an hour or so, sometimes talking although my mind was in other places and I can't honestly recall a single thing that was said. Although the sex was over, I was still slightly incredulous at the concept of this unorthodox little party going on in my room and it was nice to have a little time to wind down gradually rather than them just getting up and heading straight off.

Eventually, of course, they had to leave and, although I was sad to see them go, I confess I was quite looking forward to the opportunity to run the events of that evening through my mind once more, before the afterglow had passed. I walked them to their car and waved them off, returning to collapse, exhausted, on the sofa with a large glass of wine in my hand and very large smile on my face as various scenarios replayed through my head. It had been a fantastic evening but aside from messaging them to thank them for coming over and to check they made it home, I didn't get in touch again or suggest a second meet. I've no idea whether they would have been interested in getting together again anyway, but because it had been such a sublime experience, I didn't want to risk spoiling the memory if a second session hadn't lived up to expectation. I preferred, selfishly, to box that one up and keep it, unsullied, in all its gleaming perfection.

It occurred to me to be pleased that I felt that way. To be happy that there were experiences I could have now which I could enjoy and treasure the memory of without feeling that customary, overwhelming pang of guilt that they didn't include Lynn. It probably wasn't the most standard form of progression through the challenges of dealing with grief but, in its own way, I could see it as such for me. Now that I'd had enough encounters to offset my immediate needs and was comfortable in the knowledge that there would be others if I wanted them, I could stop simply focussing on where the next physical release might be coming from and take a step back to consider where this was all taking me on other levels too. Relieved as I was to divest myself of the raging sexual frustration I'd been feeling for so long, I was wary of becoming too dependent on the thrill of successive new partners. It was still new territory for me and, although not a particularly cautious person by nature, I didn't want to just get swept along on the excitement and novelty without giving the potential consequences at least some thought.

Looking at it as objectively as possible, I tried to assess the benefits and downsides of continuing down this path. Certainly, there were evident and obvious plus points, not only in terms of some of the situations I'd found myself in, but also in my general state of mind. It suddenly struck me that, aside from the swinging encounters, without conscious effort, I'd started engaging much more with the people around me, had been far more proactive in making arrangements to go out with friends and hadn't spent nearly so much time cowering under the threat that my paralysing grief would descend upon me again. All distinctly positive changes, I felt, which had gradually, imperceptibly, asserted themselves over the past six months. So far, so good.

I looked for the negatives. Certainly that slightly uncomfortable sense of doing something which I knew might be generally *'disapproved of'* was a lingering one. Despite the lack of issue when my neighbours had become aware of it, I did stop to wonder what my family, friends and wider acquaintances would make of it if they ever found out. The potential loss of my lovely friends was not a happy thought, although, realistically, I doubted they would react quite that badly. Family was another matter. God only knew what they would make of it. However, this was all speculation and even I could see that it was a bit pointless to spend much time worrying about it or to let that worry affect my decisions.

In terms of future potential relationships, I had to acknowledge that it might be a little off-putting to a girl to discover that I had this sort of history behind me. That aside, the more important concern was whether this lifestyle might open me up to the idea of engaging in a monogamous relationship at some point in the future or whether it might possibly sever my attachment to the idea of one completely. It's not that wanting such a relationship was entirely the goal of all this, but I felt the need to at least leave myself with the option.

In the end, I decided that the fact I was aware of the potential effects and able to think rationally about them probably meant that I was still fundamentally okay. Also, it seemed to me that the unquestionable increase in optimism and my general sense of well-being was a good enough reason to continue in its own right. In any case, I had to acknowledge that all this pondering was academic really, since I was having far too much of a good time to leave it all behind quite yet.

David B

Not Every One's a Winner

So, my journey was well underway now, with enough successful encounters under my belt for my confidence and optimism to have grown immeasurably. After the resounding success of my latest series of meets, I felt I was on a roll, a roll I didn't want to break or interrupt if I could possibly avoid it. Naturally enough, though, as soon as you start to relax a little, life has a tendency to throw a few curve balls into the mix just in case you were getting complacent. I suppose I shouldn't have been too surprised, then, that my very next meet was, disappointingly, an utter waste of time and an unwelcome reminder of the less glorious side of swinging.

I had agreed to meet with another couple 'Mr & Mrs H', at what they described as their 'holiday home' on the coast. It had a pleasant ring to it so I agreed to go there, without a prior meet, and actually had a very enjoyable drive down through the countryside, on a beautiful June evening, feeling a sense of eager anticipation at the prospect of a satisfying and pleasurable time ahead. Arriving at the address they'd given me, I realised that the 'holiday home' was actually a static caravan on a camp site and, sadly, not a particularly salubrious looking camp site either. Putting that minor disappointment to one side, I kept my hopes up and tried not to let the run-down look of the place put me off. I parked up and eventually found what I thought was the right caravan. Through the chintzy net curtains at the window, illuminated on the inside, I could see what I assumed was Mrs H, sat down, sideways on to my view of her. She didn't immediately appeal from that angle but as first impressions go, it was hardly a fair one to judge her on. She was sipping from a large glass of wine and one of those definitely had appeal, so

I knocked at the door, at least hopeful of some palatable refreshment and ready to see where this evening would lead.

Unfortunately, on meeting Mrs H face to face, it seemed that the gently filtering effect of the net curtains had set her in quite a flattering light. She was not well blessed in the looks department and I was suddenly disappointed to be driving since it occurred to me that more alcohol than I was going to be allowed might be necessary to overcome my gut response. However, I counselled myself to give it some time and headed in to meet Mr H. They were both certainly older and considerably larger than their profile had suggested, a fact which annoyed me slightly and didn't exactly get us off to a great start. Nonetheless, having made the effort to drive this far, I acquiesced and accepted their offer of a glass of wine, trying hard to conceal the growing desperation of need I was feeling for one. They then announced that they'd also invited a friend of theirs to join us, 'Mr G', who would be along in a while, a potential scenario they hadn't so much as mentioned that they were considering, let alone cleared with me prior to my arrival, which seemed rather ill-mannered in the circumstances. To make matters worse, Mr G, without whom we were apparently unable to get started, had been delayed by an hour due to traffic, leaving me to endure the deeply uninspiring company of the less-than-comely Mrs H and her, I'm sorry to say, rather gormless husband, with only a glass of what appeared to be paint-stripper for sustenance.

The painfully long-awaited and, sadly, equally gormless Mr G finally arrived eventually and, having established that his addition to the party was not going to inject the hoped-for level of vivacity or interest which would have made the encounter tolerable, I made my excuses and left as quickly as possible. To this day, I don't really know what they had in mind for that particular session but with three guys present to just one woman, and not the most appealing of women either, I didn't feel inclined to hang around long enough to find out.

Oh well. You win some, you lose some. I tried not to let it put me off my stride.

The following meet, just a few days later, I'm pleased to say, got off to a rather better start. Sabrina and I met for a drink on a Saturday night at The Shepherd and Flock pub in Farnham. She was certainly attractive, although, again, rather larger than she had implied on her profile, but with a lively personality and a good sense of humour. She hadn't had any verifications so I'd taken a bit of a chance on her but we all have to start somewhere and the initial impressions were very promising all round.

We seemed to be enjoying one another's company so, once we'd finished our drinks, I suggested retreating to my place. To my surprise, she got up rather hastily, muttered an excuse and departed. I was a little perplexed but had no option but to accept of her lack of inclination to proceed. Twenty-four hours later, her profile had been deleted and I can only assume that she was just exploring the scene and had decided it wasn't for her. I'm pretty sure I hadn't said anything untoward so I really hope it wasn't something I did that frightened her off.

Everyone, of course, whether on this scene or not, obviously has the right to opt out of any situation at any time. I totally respect that. At least the evening was an enjoyable one, even if it didn't result in the hoped-for physical pleasures but, to be honest, I had assumed that people putting themselves up on that website were people who were pretty confident they knew what they wanted out of it.

Hot in the Kitchen Tonight

After two disappointing experiences in a row, I took a little break to regroup before delving back into the websites again. When I logged back in, I was rewarded for my brief absence with the sight of a number of newly listed profiles and I was soon messaging several prospects. One stood out in particular: Tessa, a girl in her late twenties who appeared to be very pretty and petite. I wasn't especially hopeful of a meet, especially since she was based in Kent, quite a long drive away but, to my surprise, the distance didn't seem much of an issue to her and it was no more than a few days and a handful of emails before we had agreed to get together.

I offered to drive over to her or to meet her somewhere halfway between us, whatever suited best, but her preference was to come to my house. Her messages seemed very upbeat, in fact she seemed positively eager to get things underway. Allowing myself to be slightly optimistic but unwilling to let my hopes get too high after recent events, I awaited her appearance with what I hoped was an open mind. As I opened the door on the appointed day, she pretty much walked in and, somehow negotiating Milton's lolloping form and whiskery greeting, started kissing me up against the wall almost before I could get the door closed behind her. Fantastic! I can't help but love a woman who's prepared to take control every now and then. When she came up for air I took the opportunity to offer her a cup of tea but it was all I could do to get the kettle filled and on before she was enthusiastically flinging herself at me again. Giving in to her insistent kisses and my own masculine urges, I abandoned the tea in favour of some fairly impassioned snogging and groping. Her beguiling sense of urgency was having a profoundly obvious

97

effect on my appendage and it wasn't long before she was reaching down to release the beast whilst I concentrated on exploring her delicately small but perfectly formed breasts. Carried away now by the rapid flow of this encounter I all but tore off her jeans, lifted her on to the edge of the worktop and let my tongue loose on her, working round her cute silky underwear and revelling in her ability to enjoy the moment in such an uninhibited way. Taking my head between her hands she brought me up onto my feet and kissed me deeply, before sliding off the worktop, grabbing her bag and leading me upstairs. Utterly won over by her forthright style, I followed, like a lamb to the slaughter.

Thereafter followed an hour or more of intense and highly imaginative sex. Like some kind of minxy Mary Poppins, from her bag she pulled a seemingly endless array of toys and was helpfully instructive about what she'd like me to do with them. She was pretty keen on the alternative use of the back door, as it were, and wanted me to explore that whole area, after she'd warmed up, with some lubed dildoes and simultaneous shagging and butt-plug penetration. I loved it all and could have gone on all afternoon, losing count of the number of times she orgasmed. I've never, before or since, been asked to stop but she did, eventually, ask for a breather. While she recovered, I popped back downstairs to re-boil the kettle intent on finally producing the tea I'd promised her earlier. When I returned, however, she was sound asleep on the bed so I covered her over and left her to nap while I sat downstairs and switched on the TV. It was pleasing, if slightly surreal, watching rugby on the telly, knowing that there was a contentedly snoozing sex kitten upstairs in my bed. After an hour or so, though, I thought I'd better check she was ok.

She stirred as I entered the room so I climbed back into bed with her and we chatted a little while she woke up fully. I wouldn't have been surprised if she'd had enough for one

day but, after a few minutes, she started touching and stroking me, just gently, almost idly at first but before long her
grip became stronger, more intense, bringing me zinging
back to life before, with a grin, she sank below the covers to
continue her mission orally. Before long, we were at it again.
Not so much use of the toys this time, but still, we had another fantastic session culminating in one final, audibly satisfactory orgasm for her before she returned me to her mouth,
working me until I exploded within, another irrepressible
grin on her face as she swallowed me up.

Concerned that she was now faced with quite a long drive, I
reminded her that she was welcome to stay the night if she
was tired but she opted to head straight home. Probably not
a bad call since I suspect that, had she stayed with me, she
wouldn't have been a whole lot less tired come the morning
in any case. I did manage to persuade her to let me fix her
something to eat and drink before she left though. Perching
on the worktop where the fun had all started that afternoon,
she chattered away animatedly as I got some supplies together, eventually heading off into the night with strict instructions to message me and let me know when she arrived
home safely.

Wow, what a great girl! She'd certainly shown me a thing or
two and I couldn't have wished for a more thorough
workout. A damned shame she lived so far away, it would
have been fun to further my education with her.

David B

I Ain't MissCing You

Optimism now renewed, I wasted little time in getting back on the website to see who else was around and who might want a playdate.

Amongst the stream of profiles, I spotted a very promising looking one put up by a single woman in her thirties. She looked very attractive and her profile was appealing so I got in touch and had a pretty welcoming reply. We ended up chatting online for quite a while that evening and eventually she suggested meeting up. The success of my previous encounter had encouraged me to let down my guard and I, perhaps a little too hastily, offered my place as a venue without the a prior meet. But she looked and sounded lovely so in a warmly non-defensive moment I took a chance.

Big mistake.

Miss C had obviously used photos taken several, if not many, years ago; a basic trick which I had fallen victim to before. She was also very chubby, I would say, clinically, bordering on obese, which is fine so long as you are going to be honest about it. She hadn't been honest though and, unfortunately, I just didn't find this version of her in the least bit attractive. Mistake number two was that I'd offered to have her stay over for the night so that she wouldn't have to worry about getting home. I still feel a bit sheepish about this one and am sitting here cringing a little as I write so I'm not going to dwell too long. Although her appearance took me by surprise, she was pleasant enough and we did have quite a nice conversation while I cooked dinner. Once at the table, however, my mood changed when I saw her eat. Let's just say I should have given her a shovel rather than a knife and fork. It was not a pretty sight.

So I drank.

A lot.

What else could I do?

Once we'd had dinner and the horrible reality had dawned fully upon me, she'd had too much to drink for me to suggest she drive home. I tried to consume sufficient quantities to put the old chap to sleep, as well as my brain, but the dirty bugger resisted sedation and in the end, when I couldn't put it off any longer, we trooped (well, I trooped, she sort of lumbered like a partially tranquilised rhino) upstairs. The deed was performed but my mind is resisting bringing up the memory in any great detail. I wanted her to go the minute it was over but, thanks to my own misjudgement, I was treated to a brief period of clinging to the edge of the bed while she floundered around in the rest of it, grunting and snoring like some great whale-pig. When I could take no more, I sought sanctuary on the sofa but, although I'd escaped the constant thrashing of her restless form, I could still hear her from there.

It was hell.

Come the morning, I was woken by her thudding down the stairs and felt obliged to make some excuse about feeling unwell when she asked why I was on the sofa. I said I had to leave soon as I was going off to visit my parents but really I just wanted to get her out and away from me as quickly as possible.

David B

A few days later I had a text from Miss C asking if I'd like to make it a regular thing or even a relationship.

Oh my god! No way!

Quite apart from not finding her at all attractive and still being rather cross about her misleading me, one of the reasons I joined the swingers brigade was to avoid that kind of pressure and if there was one thing for certain, I never, ever wanted to have to watch her troughing or listen to that horrendous snoring again. My experience with Miss C had, if nothing else, taught me a lesson about going online wearing beer goggles and an alcohol brain filter.

To add to my downturn in mood, within days my beloved Milton, at a creditable fourteen years old, chose his moment to depart this world having succumbed to a major stroke. With his passing, I lost my loyal and devoted buddy of so many years, one I had, of course, shared with Lynn too, which added to the poignancy of his loss. I felt his absence very deeply, being forced, on some levels, to revisit emotions which still had quite a raw edge and face them down again. I confess, it floored me for a while, driving me back into my shell for a period of time while I rode the waves of those rather unwelcome emotions until the storm had passed. During that time, I didn't feel at all inclined to put myself back out there and it was several weeks before I logged on to any of the websites again.

Interstellar

Once things had settled down a bit after the loss of Milton, I began to think about looking online at potential encounters again but didn't feel up to taking on anything too intense or complicated. On one of my favourite swinging sites, you can carry out a search using your postcode to find potential meets nearby. I'd been amazed to find people there from my own village, especially as it's a small, seemingly quiet place where you really wouldn't think much of this sort of thing was going on at all. Vaguely wondering if there was a suitable option near at hand, I logged into the site and had another look down the list of profiles for people in the area. It is always slightly intriguing to look, knowing you might recognise a person or two. On one occasion, I'd come across a couple I remembered as having been work colleagues of Lynn's. It had made me stop and smile but I hadn't felt inclined to connect with them. It was a sunny Sunday morning, so I sat in the garden with my tea and toast, idly scanning through the current list. There were actually five or six profiles listed in the area and I scanned through these one by one to see what was on offer. In the end, I only really felt drawn to one of them, so I decided to make contact and see what happened.

Her name was Stella and it turned out that she lived barely half a mile away from my house. She was in her early fifties and in a long-term relationship with someone who was already married to someone else. That person wasn't aware that his lover was also making herself available on this particular website but, since he was having an affair with her in the first place, I suppose he wouldn't really have had much right to complain. Her profile stated that she absolutely loved giving blow jobs, to the point of being quite obsessed with it and regularly making herself available at 'Glory Holes'. In case explanation is needed, these are venues where a woman will sit on one side of a partition with a hole in it and give oral attention to any male appendage that appears through the hole. Neither the man nor the woman knows who the other is or what they might look like so there is a retained element of mystery. I can see why that might appeal on a certain level but I must admit it's not something that I've ever felt inclined to seek out. I'm not entirely sure why that is but I'm very visually orientated and the sight of a woman doing that to me forms a big part of my enjoyment. I think, also, at the back of my mind, there is the slight fear factor involved in not knowing who is attending to you. Potentially someone you'd find grotesquely unattractive, maybe another bloke even. Not something I personally relish the thought of.

My message was, I must confess, despatched with slightly half-hearted intention since I was still feeling a bit low and listless after my weeks in the doldrums, but she responded within the hour with a pleasant, slightly humorous reply which perked me up and led to a few rapid email exchanges. We established that our mutual needs were well suited and, since neither of us was otherwise engaged, we agreed to meet at my house that very evening. No pre-meeting with this one but, since she lived so close by, it seemed a bit of a waste of time as if we didn't want to take things further she could, rather conveniently, just potter off home again.

Stella arrived at about half past seven. On first impression, she had a lovely, warm feel about her, red hair perfectly setting off her twinkly grey-green eyes. Lovely smile too. I brought wine through to the sitting room and we sat together, chatting easily until, with barely half a glass of wine inside her, she reached over and casually unzipped me. That slightly caught me unawares but the audacity also amused me. I grinned and continued to sip my wine, making some pretence at keeping up a conversation, though my attention was noticeably slipping. I watched as she slid her hand deeper, feeling her way through the layers. My almost instant response to her attentions made her quarry easy to find and extract. We remained like this for a while, her hand cruising the length of me, occasionally delving back inside my jeans to cup and stroke my balls too. Although the sensation was electrifying certain parts of my body, oddly, I also felt an utter sense of calm and relaxation, akin to the feeling you might get when you give yourself over to a highly skilled therapist at a spa. I was clearly in very safe and experienced hands, utterly content to sit back and let her administer her treatment, magically dissipating the accumulated stress and tension of the past weeks.

Slowly, she leaned her whole body towards me, bending over me to eventually make contact, lip to tip. The anticipation was so great by this time, that the first touch was almost like a little electric shock which sent corresponding ripples surging through me. The sensation was unexpectedly intense and if I hadn't been in such a sublimely relaxed state I might have unloaded there and then. Well, I suppose it had been a while!

Rolling herself off the edge of the sofa to kneel between my legs, Stella quietly pulled the top of my jeans down a little to fully free me, then, moving in close, she started to suck. And, oh my lord, could she suck! She could probably contribute a fair bit to Dyson's Research and Development department. I guess it must have been a combination of natural talent and all that practice but this was a seriously gifted woman. She was also one of the very few women I have had the pleasure to enjoy who could properly deep throat. It was sensational and just incredible to watch. Her profound expertise meant that it was just minutes before I was starting to tingle uncontrollably, feeling the impending surge. She glanced up at me, making eye contact and within seconds I was coming in massive bursts of blessed release while Stella moaned contentedly swallowing it all down as I watched her throat expanding and contracting while I lay still buried deep within. What an amazing feeling. This lifestyle certainly has its highs and lows, like anything else, but that was most definitely one of the higher highs.

The fact that I stay hard after coming for the first time seems to surprise (hopefully pleasantly) most of the women who have noticed it. Stella was no exception. So pleased, in fact, was she to see me still so hard in the aftermath that after a few minutes chatting and some gentle stroking she decided that she was still hungry and down she went again, working her unique brand of magic but paying more attention to my balls this time, taking them in her mouth one at a time and rolling them around. Perhaps she hadn't been joking when she'd said she was hungry as she had a bit of chew on one - that certainly made my eyes water. She almost had me worried for a moment. Getting back into her stride, she took me fully down once again, a sight and sensation I doubt I could ever tire of. Before long she had brought me back to the brink and I watched in awestruck admiration as a second dose of my man juice worked its way down her throat. Once she'd disengaged herself, we reclined contentedly on the sofa chatting amicably while finished off our wine. I couldn't help but tell her how amazed and impressed I was with her abilities but she just shrugged and gave me a salacious little smile.

Needless to say, it had been tremendously satisfying to meet Stella, exactly what I had needed to re-energise me and drag me back up to the surface. She was fabulous, a true master of her art, and I did consider inviting her round again a few times over the following months but at that stage, despite my immediate neighbours having become aware, I was still trying to keep my activities generally below the radar. I live in such a small village that it seemed a little risky in case she was well known and people in the wider community realised what I was up to. It seems a bit silly now, of course, as I am quite open about my lifestyle and no longer make any great effort to conceal things.

In any case, given how close we live to one another, I expected to run into her from time to time but, surprisingly, I haven't seen her even once. Possibly she was keeping her head down and avoiding me for the same reasons, although she'd given me the impression of being quite up front about it all. She had told me that she was considering moving to Wales so if she's moved on that would explain it. I'm quite certain she will be finding herself extremely popular, wherever she is.

David B

One, Two, Three

My next encounter was with a lovely couple, Don and Janice, who lived just outside Petersfield. They had a fairly standard profile, nothing too hard-core, which looked like the sort of thing that I usually found suited me and was likely to progress. I was still firing off messages pretty regularly to potential profiles just to keep the flow going, since, obviously, not every message sent gets a response or progresses. Occasionally, this policy would lead to a bit of a bottleneck but since the worst that could happen was a glut of sex encounters I was quite happy with that anyway.

Don and Janice had both been married before, were both divorced and had been together for a couple of years. Don had been on the swinging scene with his former wife and had introduced the concept to Janice who, fortunately for them both, had taken to it like the proverbial duck to water and they had been swinging together for a while before I met them. I'm always just a little bit wary when I meet with couples as I want to feel sure that they both actively want to be involved with the whole thing as I've sometimes come across people who I deduce are being goaded into the situation by their partner or are just there to try to keep a relationship going under threat that it will be over if they don't comply. This makes me incredibly sad and is, I suppose, one of the downsides of what I do. However, it's easy enough to spot warning signs and if I suspect that's what's happening I will just make my excuses and take the encounter no further. It's sometimes tempting to get involved and state my opinion, particularly if it is the woman who seems reticent as I instinctively feel quite protective, but as you have so little background to go on and I'm very aware there are many sides to every story, I feel it's safest to keep a distance and just quietly leave the scene. You never know what damage you might inadvertently do, don't know whether, perhaps, you might make a situation worse rather than better. We are adults, after all, and entitled to make our own decisions about how we live this aspect of our lives.

In any case, I was immediately put at ease on meeting this couple for an initial drink. They just seemed incredibly relaxed and happy, very comfortable, both with each other and with the situation, so I had no concerns there at all. In fact, they were very pleasant company, the sort of people you couldn't help but like and relax around. We chatted and laughed through just one drink before I suggested they come back to mine for a play. They seemed perfectly happy to do that and in no time at all we were off, driving through the darkness to my cosy cottage, scene of so many of my encounters. Wine was poured when we arrived but, although we took it upstairs with us, we'd barely touched it before we were all getting undressed, laughing and completely unselfconscious.

Janice nuzzled her nice, curvy body up to me and started kissing me while Don finished undressing then sat nearby and watched, every so often reaching in to stroke or fondle whichever part of Janice was exposed at the time. They were interacting with each other almost the whole time in one way or another, exchanging comments, touching or kissing while I was doing whatever I happened to be doing to Janice at the same time. They involved me in their banter too, though, and it felt like a very cosy threesome indeed. Whilst I was indulging Janice in a little light cunnilingus, Don was tending to her breasts until I, at Janice's request, came to kneel above her face so that she could have access to me orally. So Don and I swapped ends and while I was enjoying the feel of Janice's hands and tongue, Don got out a dildo they'd brought with them and started using it on her. That seemed to fire her up quite well resulting in me getting quite frenzied attention from her in turn to the point where it was getting almost too intense to bear and I needed to ease back a bit. She responded by grabbing me by the shoulders and pretty much forcing me down until I was lying on top of her. She then neatly rolled me over and in one movement was astride me, teasing me by sliding back and forth over me before easing down on me in stages while bringing Don up onto his knees so she could suck him at the same time. It was seamlessly controlled. I was impressed.

I reached down and caressed her bum as her ample breasts jiggled about just in front of my face, easing my head up to catch her nipples whenever I could reach. Don had his hands in her hair, looking adoringly at her as she sucked contentedly away at him. Everyone was happy; I could just lie back, relax, and lose myself in all the sensations of skin and movement. Inevitably, the moment eventually built to a climax, Janice's first, thankfully, as I wasn't sure how much longer I could have held out for her, trapped as I was and completely at her mercy. Relieved to feel her writhing and sighing through her orgasm, I succumbed to my own pleasure before relinquishing her to Don who gave her a bit of recovery time before taking his turn and making her come again as he got his release too.

Then we just lay there and chilled out, chatting away, and it all seemed so utterly natural. Gently, Don suggested to Janice that it was time they thought about getting home and she began to extricate herself and find her clothes. There was no hurry, no sudden rush, no sense of 'time's up', which you get with some people. It was a fantastic experience from start to finish and I really hoped to see them again.

As with normal dating, there's the slight inclination to do the 'I'll call you' thing at the end, whether you intend to see the other person (or people) again or not, but with this couple I actually felt certain I would see them again and was thinking how nice it would be to make this a regular thing. It's a slight conundrum in the swinging world that you're all in it for the variety and non-commitment but there is still appeal, to some degree, in finding people you can have on-going meets with just because it takes away the issues of the unknown quantity, i.e. not knowing whether you will like the person you are going to meet, at least enough to have sex with them, whether or not you're perhaps going to find that they've failed to disclose some vital gem of information such as they weigh twenty stone, need to stop for a cigarette every six minutes, have had a sex change or perhaps have a history of psychotic illness. In fairness, most of the people I have encountered haven't exhibited any of these issues, of course, but there's always the possibility lurking there so it's nice to have meets where you know more or less what you're in for.

So we parted ways with hugs all round and what I felt were sincere words about keeping in touch and meeting again soon. I waved them off and, after a celebratory nightcap, went back to bed a contented man. As is my custom, I sent them both a text the next day to thank them for coming over and say how much I'd enjoyed their company. I had a chatty response from them both via Janice's number with a 'see you again very soon' sign off. A couple of weeks later I sent them a message, asking if they were up for putting a date in the diary to meet again. I didn't hear back so left it a week or so before sending another message in case they hadn't got the first. This time I did get a very apologetic response explaining that they had decided to get married and were not likely to be available for a while as they'd both had to take on second jobs in order to get some money together.

I was quite surprised at my inner response to that as I felt nothing but happy for them, not a single pang or twinge of jealousy, and so I was able to send them a genuinely congratulatory response wishing them well and encouraging them to get back in touch at any time in the future as and when the opportunity and inclination arose. Then, having plenty of other options in the offing, simply moved on.

It might seem strange to report feelings of happiness for a newly engaged couple since that, of course, would generally be a normal response, but it was simply the fact that I could enjoy such a thing without any backlash of self pity, without even a slight ripple of decline in my own mood. It was a definite step forward and gave me a sense of hope.

Maggie. May I...?

Restored to my former levels of interest by my encounters with Don and Janice and with Stella, I had sent out a handful of messages to some of the newer profiles as well as a few to people who were based farther away than I might have considered before. These led to a meet with a sweet girl who was brand new to the scene and had needed a fair bit of reassurance but which had ended most successfully. From the messages sent further afield, I had several responses, one of which led to perhaps the most bizarre and challenging encounter I ever got involved with.

The scenario took place over the period of about eight weeks, starting in the early autumn. It was with a married couple, Maggie and Tom, who lived in Kent. From her photographs, Maggie seemed attractive in a 'natural beauty' kind of way and also appeared to be quite a bit younger than her husband. Their profile stated quite emphatically that they were seeking a 'bull' for a cuckold relationship, which, for the uninitiated, is where a man is brought in to openly take the wife, or female partner, from the man in the existing relationship. This is designed to give rise to conflicting and heightened emotions for all parties and was not something I'd really been aware of beforehand but I did a little research and thought I'd probably got enough of an idea to give it a try. As Tom and Maggie lived so far away I wasn't particularly expecting a positive response to my message, but was pleased and more than a little intrigued when they did reply. A three-way conversation ensued over the next few days that eventually led to us arranging to meet up at a small pub local to them.

113

David B

It was nearly a two-hour drive, which gave me plenty of time to turn the cuckold concept over in my head and wonder how 'bullish' I needed to be. I really had very little idea how this meet was going to play out. I found the pub easily enough, taking a moment to gather my thoughts before heading through the car park in the early evening to find my way inside. They were already ensconced and both, thankfully, easily recognisable from their photos. I introduced myself and settled down beside them for an hour or so of chatting, which was both productive and unusually informative. I was glad I hadn't needed to jump straight into role-play but within that hour I felt I'd got a good enough grasp of what they wanted from me. It seemed I had a decision to make. 'Well, I've driven all this way', I thought, 'might as well take the bull by the horns' and, having nothing to lose, I decided to show my hand and make an open play for Maggie.

So I came straight out and said 'Maggie, I like you. I like you very much. I think you are an incredibly sexy, beautiful woman and I really want to take you home and fuck you but what I want you to do first is go to the ladies' room, remove your underwear and undo your blouse so I can see your cleavage. Then I want you to come back out here and put your underwear on the table so that I, and everyone else here, can see what you've done'.

Without a word or a moment's hesitation, she got up and headed off across the pub, returning a few minutes later, underwear in hand, giving me a smile before placing it on the table, in full view, as I had directed. It did raise an eyebrow or two. As I recall, it was half price fish and chips night for pensioners so the place was quite busy and our antics were not the sort of thing that this clientele were used to. I'm not particularly exhibitionist by nature but, since it was highly unlikely that I'd ever see any of these locals again, I went with it, finding the whole thing both intriguing and slightly amusing. After continuing with general conversation for another fifteen minutes or so, whilst trying in vain to keep our eyes off Maggie's knickers laying so obviously on the table, we decided a change of venue was in order, paid the bill and headed off toward their house which was just a few miles away.

As soon as we were indoors, Maggie launched herself at me and started kissing me like a crazed animal. Slightly surprised but very pleased not to have to work my way through any further preamble, I responded in kind and we remained locked together for some time, our hands roaming all over one another. Reaching under her skirt I slid a finger to the top of her thigh, a charge jolting through me when I explored between her legs and found her already wet. Glad to have dispensed with her underwear earlier, I freely slid my fingers back and forth in the slippery juices, dropping my mouth to her nipples when she pulled her blouse to one side, scooping out and offering her delectable breast to me. Slowly, I made my way down her body, savouring the feeling of a hot, intensely horny, gorgeous woman on the tip of my tongue. For the next two hours we were licking and sucking and fucking in the lounge, kitchen and bedroom with Tom appearing now and again but not really seeming to be watching all that much which made me wonder, briefly, what was really in it for him. We finished up in the bedroom, both naked, Maggie wedged up against the wall, me supporting her thighs whilst I pummelled her for all I was worth. I'm not sure who needed the release more, her or me. There seemed to be equal parts of frantic, energetic desire on both sides and it was an electrifyingly fantastic session which left me exhausted but utterly exhilarated. Tom offered to make coffee before I left but I declined, preferring to drift away, still hazy and lost in my blissful post-coital glow for the duration of the drive home.

The following day, once I'd settled a little, I reflected on the whole scenario and still couldn't work out what was in it for

David B

Tom. I wondered if it just hadn't worked out for him and he'd let Maggie get on with things so as not to spoil it for her. I certainly wouldn't have been surprised if that had been as far as it all went but I suppose it must have been deemed a satisfactory arrangement fort hem both because it wasn't long before they were back in touch and suggesting another meet. And so, a couple of weeks after that first session, I found myself making my way back to Kent once more. Not so fortunate with traffic this time, I had a terrible journey and didn't arrive until 8:30, nearly an hour later than planned. I rang the bell, preparing to apologise for my lateness as the door was opened. Instead, my jaw dropped slightly as I was confronted with the vision of Tom, silhouetted in the door-way, wearing a light blue dress and women's high-heeled shoes. I hope it would be fair to say that I'm generally open minded about things and I certainly don't have a problem with people cross-dressing, although I've never felt com-pelled to try it for myself, but the unexpectedness of the sight took me by surprise. I don't judge these things though and regained my composure very quickly, hoping he hadn't noticed my initial reaction.

Tom nodded a brief welcome then stood back to allow me inside, informing me that Maggie was in the kitchen before ushering me on through. Maggie turned to greet me and, for the second time in as many minutes, I was stopped dead in my tracks. She was looking absolutely stunning in a slinky, silky, dark blue dress which showed off her petite figure and her tumbling, dark blonde hair to perfection. She'd looked pretty good the first time we'd met but this evening she ap-peared to have made rather more effort and with impressive results. I breathed in and took a moment just to admire her before giving voice to what had been going on in my head up to that point about how she looked. She beamed a smile at me as she approached, kissing my cheek before placing a large glass of wine in one hand, taking me firmly by the other and leading me straight upstairs to the bedroom.

116

By the time I'd taken a couple of sips, she had unzipped her dress and turned to stand before me, raising her arms, almost childlike, so I could peel it off her. I did as silently requested, draping the dress over the back of a chair but keeping my eyes on her the whole time. She looked radiant, positively glowing, in her skimpy, lacy underwear, sexy, heeled shoes still on, elongating her frame. Mental snapshots captured for my rainy day file, I, almost reluctantly, not wanting to alter this goddess vision before me, reached out to gently touch, then remove, her final layers before guiding her onto the bed. Discarding my own clothes as un-clumsily as possible, I laid alongside her, still mesmerised, slowly running my hands over every inch of her. Marvelling at the silky smoothness of her skin, I traced her cheekbones, caressed her neck, cupped and kissed her peachy breasts then religiously travelled every one of her gloriously feminine lines. I was captivated. So absorbed, in fact, that I had forgotten completely about Tom, utterly unaware, with my back to the door, that he had, at some point, followed us into the room. Oblivious, I continued my pilgrimage around Maggie's body, fingers eventually finding their way to the Mecca that was her divine tightness, sliding back and forth, back and forth, in her juices before requesting sanctuary.

She had been breathing more and more heavily throughout my progress and as soon as my fingers began to delve she arched so hard against my hand it left me in no doubt what she wanted next. Her arms, which had been delicately laid above her head on the pillows, now moved to grasp my neck and shoulders, determinedly pulling me over on top of her. I smiled and yielded to her demands, positioning myself above her in preparation for a few last, teasing moments as I prepared to plunge in. From this new position, though, I finally caught a glimpse of Tom standing slightly away from the bed, giving me a fleeting mental jolt as I processed the sight. It didn't take me long to adjust - I'd been 'watched' quite a number of times now so it was nothing very new - however, now aware of his presence, my peripheral vision had a lock on him and I was slightly distracted when he, having observed us for a few more moments, slowly lifted the hem of his dress, reached below and began to fondle himself. I simultaneously added two pieces of information to my dossier on this couple at that moment. First, poor Tom appeared to have the smallest cock I'd ever seen, not that I'd really seen so very many at that stage but it was seriously tiny. Second, what little there was, plainly wasn't responding, at all, to any of the stimulation it was receiving.

Perhaps drawn from her reverie by my slight change of pace, Maggie swung her gaze sideways and almost immediately began yelling at Tom to leave us alone and get back downstairs. Though I'd been mildly perturbed by the sight of him standing there, it certainly wasn't bothering me a great deal so her reaction seemed a little harsh. Although they'd advertised for a specific role-play participant, I'm a great believer in all parties having an equally good time and it immediately appeared to me that Tom was not going to be having much of a good a time at all, although I could have been completely missing the point. Aware that I was a beginner with the cuckold idea, I couldn't be sure if her response was just in line with the scenario they'd got me involved to complete. So I gave him what I hoped was a cheery wink as he was turning to go, feeling a little sorry for him in all honesty, although I was soon fully focussed again on my interaction with Maggie. Tom despatched, Maggie pulled me into her with almost ferocious intensity and we energetically continued our sport. Happy not to have an audience, I banged away mercilessly away on her until I felt her stiffen and she began a noisy, prolonged orgasm. I briefly wondered if I should release too but was pretty sure she wouldn't have had enough yet. I was right. It barely seemed to break her stride and with the first throes of urgency safely managed we settled into a still intense but less frantic rhythm. I withdrew and turned her onto her side, spooning in behind her, taking her deeply, bending her almost double to get as hard in as I could. Her small, firm body was lithe and supple, delicate but strong; the sort of body which has you in awe that something so little and perfectly formed could be so resilient as you're driving into it like your life depended on it. Breathtakingly sexy.

Keeping myself wedged firmly in place, I rolled her on to her front and continued ploughing away as she lay pinned down, face buried in a pillow, moaning but unable to really move much. Using my knees, I moved her legs wider apart and then wider still, in my mind I had them tied out by the ankle, her unable to move and completely at my mercy. The angle made her toned, tight little butt cheeks tense and clench, showing them off to their maximum benefit and it looked pretty amazing from where I was seeing it. I reached up and spread her arms wide above her head too, leaning some weight on her wrists so she was completely spread-eagled, essentially powerless. I held her there as I pressed on, the tone of the sounds she was making leaving me confident that she was enjoying this as much as I was. Long, deep, penetrating strokes, over and over, until my body eventually started to quake with the effort of maintaining the position and pace, so tempted to change position again but persisting determinedly as I felt her starting to quiver once more, the pitch of her moans rising with her impending orgasm. As she came, I kept my grip on her, pressing her hard and flat into the bed as her surprisingly strong body arched back against the resistance. The energy coming off her was amazing and the feeling of power from holding her down had me on the point of climaxing too. I resisted though, more through sheer exhaustion than self-control, and instead, once she'd done, I rolled her over and dropped my cock towards her mouth. Eyes slightly hazy, she reached up to grasp me and brought me easily back to the brink with her mouth and hands until I disgorged all over her pretty mouth and chin.

Spent, I dropped onto the bed beside her as she smeared my come over her breasts, eyes locked to me, before licking her sticky fingers with long, smiling strokes of her tongue. She truly was on fire that night. That was so damned erotic to watch and the exhausted but ever-attentive, still half-hard chap even stirred at the sight. Knowing she was having an impact, Maggie continued her saucy baiting though I suggested he might not be ready for any more action for a while after the beating he'd just taken. I hadn't meant it as a challenge but that's how Maggie took it. She began to wriggle and writhe in front of me, cupping her breasts and pushing them together, sliding a hand tantalisingly down her belly and burying it between her legs. Though my body was begging me to lie down and have nice post-coital nap, my mind was being drawn relentlessly back to life and, with a little of Maggie's dexterous handling to get him fully fit again, so was the little soldier. Triumphantly, Maggie sat astride me, sensuously sliding me in and out, smiling, revelling in her victory. I let her enjoy her moment before flipping her over, kneeling between her legs and pulling her hips high as she arched up to meet me.

It was about ten thirty when we finally went back downstairs. Heading for the kitchen in search of wine, it crossed my mind to wonder if we might find Tom rather less than ecstatic to see us. On the contrary, it seemed that Tom had had the foresight to order a takeaway and was patiently waiting for us to emerge so that we could all eat together. Not what I'd expected and somewhat surreal as dinner parties go but, actually, perfect. Although Tom wasn't exactly effusive towards us, he seemed to be fine which put my slightly wary mind more at ease. The much appreciated food gave me the energy reserves I needed for the night ahead too and thank god for that as I don't know how many times or for how many hours we must have played during the night. I had to be up in good time the next morning, needing to leave by eight o'clock, and it was punishing getting up at that time on virtually no sleep and after such a physically demanding night. I was exhausted but also euphoric, suddenly aware when I returned from the bathroom how fantastically strongly the whole room stank of sex. It wasn't until I was leaving that it crossed my mind to wonder about Tom. I suppose he must have stayed in the spare room overnight but I could hear sounds emanating from the kitchen whilst I dressed. As I left, he said goodbye in a friendly enough manner when I passed him on the stairs as he was apparently taking up a cup of tea for Maggie.

I'd had a fantastic night but, again, I wouldn't have been surprised if that had been an end to our involvement as I couldn't quite shake the niggling feeling that if I was Tom I'd have had just about enough by now. However, I had emails from them that same day and there was an ongoing conversation for several days afterward. It seemed that they were fine with how our arrangement was working out but I became aware that things were about to step up a gear as they obviously wanted more of the role-play type of interaction, particularly in the build up to our next meet. That was fine with me. I was very happy at the prospect of sex with Maggie again and it seemed to me that Tom was going to be much more involved which had to be a good thing for him.

Our third and final (although I didn't know it at the time) meet was on another Friday some weeks later. The difference this time was that I had been texting both Maggie and Tom. To Maggie I would text things like 'When I see you I want to fuck you whenever and wherever I like and I want you to do whatever I ask and whatever I tell you to do' in order to beef up my 'bull' role. To Tom, I would text instructions on what I wanted Maggie to wear or not wear on a daily basis and, closer to the time, specifically for our next meet. He did message me once asking me to tell him what he should wear too but I couldn't bring myself to be specific so simply said that it didn't matter to me although if he wanted to wear a dress then that was up to him and absolutely fine by me. From

121

Tuesday of the week we were due to meet, I told Maggie not to wear any knickers to work and when I was bored or horny I would send her a text telling her to go to the ladies room and finger herself or even to do it while she was sitting at her desk, and then send me a photo of herself masturbating to prove she was obeying me. I also sent messages to Tom saying that he was from now on to sleep only in the spare room, that he was not to touch Maggie and that the main bedroom was off limits to him and now reserved solely for Maggie and me. He replied saying he would observe my demands. The night before my third trip to Kent, I texted Tom with details of what I wanted Maggie to wear for the meet, namely a short skirt, see through blouse, stockings and high heels, the blouse to be unbuttoned low down so that her breasts were clearly visible. I also instructed him to write in red lipstick over Maggie's breasts 'for Dave only' and the same again just above her public line then to send me pictures to prove that he had done so.

When I arrived on the Friday evening Tom answered the door wearing a red dress and heels. Better prepared this time, I greeted him without demur and then requested that he show me through to where Maggie was waiting, in the dining room, blindfolded, as I had requested. I took a moment to enjoy the sight of her in her perfectly put together and highly revealing outfit before turning and heading straight up to 'my' bedroom, ordering Tom to bring Maggie to me in exactly five minutes' time, which he did. Leading her upstairs, still blindfolded, he brought her into the room where I was waiting, naked, already aroused and lubed. I had seen glimpses of the lipstick writing on Maggie's breasts where her low-buttoned blouse parted across her cleavage but I directed Tom to bring her over to me and pull up her skirt so I could see what he had written. The fetish thing was all pretty new to me and, as you may have surmised, I've never been greatly drawn to the concept of it but, I have to say, the sight of Maggie standing there, blindfolded, with my name written on her skin was erotic in a quite unexpected way, hinting at new levels of carnal experience I had yet to explore.

I took Maggie's arm and led her towards the foot of the bed. Pressed tightly in behind her, I guided her hands to the bedframe before reaching down and slowly sliding my hands up the outside of both her thighs, raising the skirt up over her gorgeous arse. Shuffling her legs wider apart with my feet, I drew her towards me until I was resting, throbbingly erect, between her legs and she could feel me grazing back and forth as I pushed and pulled gently on her hips. Sensing that I now had her full attention, I paused briefly, just half a beat, before thrusting straight in. She gave a sharp exhale as I entered then dropped forward a little, moaning and writhing. She spread her arms wide, grasping the frame hard and pushing back sharply against me. Utterly focused on this interplay, I was, again, completely oblivious of Tom's presence but clearly Maggie had not forgotten as, once again, without even being able to see that he was there, she began yelling at him, demanding that he get out of the room and leave us alone.

I was unaware of whether Tom had actually left or not, and, to be honest, was not bothered either way as I had almost instantly resumed full concentration, ecstatic to be, once again, fully ensconced in Maggie's deliciously enticing wetness. I continued pounding into her for some time before withdrawing, turning her to face me and pushing her down to her knees. Leaving her blindfold on, I put her hands back behind her on the bedframe and, as she swung forward I entered her mouth, moving rhythmically in and out while her lips and tongue drove me to the point of exploding. Torn between release and prolonging our session, I pulled myself back and withdrew, hauling Maggie to her feet. Sitting down on the edge of the bed, legs wide apart, I peeled off her blindfold and ordered her to finish me off. As our eyes made contact for the first time that night, she flashed me a hotly penetrating look then straddled me, taking me inside before wrapping her legs around me and leaning back, hands resting on my knees for support as she lifted away and slid back down hard onto me. Almost shockingly intense, she was unrelenting, pummelling me harder and harder, forcing me to bursting point. It was explosive. I don't believe I'd ever come so hard before. Certainly my normally ever-ready appendage was out of ammunition for a while afterwards, despite me switching Maggie on to the bed and indulging her in a similarly intense round at the mercy of my probing tongue until she had climaxed too, something which has never failed to raise his head before, however weary he may have been. Both sated at last, we lay silently together breathing heavily. Several times in the night we came together again, this new-found edginess making each session seem consumingly powerful. A different take on things and an intriguing new dimension for me, well worth the still-alien fetish game it had taken to induce it.

In the morning, Tom brought tea for us both but seemed withdrawn and noticeably failed to make eye contact with me, despite me addressing him directly at times. When he left the room Maggie voiced her opinion that he was getting more than a little jealous of us and although that was, in principle, part of the point of this whole game, I sensed that it had, perhaps, gone beyond the boundaries of his limits of acceptability. I never heard his side of the story but it would not have been at all surprising to me if he had become negative about the situation, especially since Maggie would keep telling him to leave rather than let him stay and have his voyeuristic fun too. I departed shortly afterwards to make my way back home feeling slightly shell-shocked, not to mention supremely tired. I pondered the situation during my homeward drive but came to no real conclusions except that I perhaps now had a hint of an idea what it was that people who pursued the fetish trail were after.

I dropped them an email later that day thanking them for a great night, but wasn't actually too surprised when I had no reply. Although I wasn't terribly sad to finish with the role-play thing, I was sorry not to have the prospect of further sessions with Maggie to look forward to, although the memory of this whole experience as well as those intense sessions together took quite some time to fade. I did have one more point of contact with them during the following summer when Tom sent me a text out of the blue. It seemed a slightly odd message, just asking how I was and saying hello from him and Maggie but no mention of meeting again or anything. I messaged him back asking how they both were, but never heard anything back. Perhaps they'd sent it to the wrong number and it had been meant for someone else. I guess I'll never know exactly why they discontinued our arrangement. I haven't even seen their profile online since then so I have no idea what they're up to or whether they're still swinging. From what I'd seen, Tom, hadn't got a great deal of enjoyment out of it so perhaps he'd decided he wasn't up for pursuing that route any longer.

It had been an interesting interaction all round. The sex with Maggie had been sensational and I'd certainly got a kick out of some of the pictures she'd sent me when we were in the full throes of role-play, but it wasn't something I felt inclined to actively pursue in the future. In my view it had been a bit of a pointless complication in what could have been a very simple arrangement. No doubt I was missing the point and there were many things to recommend it once you got into it but I wasn't sure I could be bothered, to be honest. Of course, I'm always open to trying new things and if something similar cropped up again, I'd just have to judge it on its merits and see what happened.

David B

Live and Let Liv

Whilst I was engaging with Maggie and Tom, I had still been active on the website and open to other meets. I began chatting to another couple who had got in touch with me via the original website. Will and Liv seemed like good prospects from their profile and the tone of their messages. She was thirty-two, he was in his early forties and they were looking for a first time M/F/M, (male/female/male) threesome. They said they'd been registered on the website for a little while, although I hadn't seen their profile before, but they told me that, thus far, the contacts they'd made had led to initial meets for drinks or coffee but gone no further. After the usual exchange of general, conversational emails, we decided to get together for early evening drinks at The George in Petersfield on the following Friday, a week after my first session with Maggie and Tom. There were no face photos on their profile so they had sent me a couple of pictures for the purposes of recognition and I'd followed my usual protocol of turning up a little early so as to get a decent table with a view of the door, allowing me to watch for their arrival. They were not long behind me, as it turned out, obviously having had a similar idea.

Will was tall and lean with dark eyes, a ready smile and a funky kind of stubbly beard of the type which looked pretty good on him but would have made me look like a hobo. Liv, similarly slim and dark eyed but, thankfully without the beard, was also very smiley and sported an amazing mass of dark, shoulder-length, almost ringlet-type curls which gave her an appealing, girlish look. Both of them had dressed casually and gave the impression of being very laid back types. They were certainly an entertaining duo too, both of them hilarious raconteurs who laughed easily and were very inclusive. I was really enjoying their company and, within the space of an hour, I felt everything seemed to be going extremely well. The atmosphere was chilled and friendly, edging increasingly towards mildly flirtatious, so I jumped right in and invited them back to my house, then left them alone for a moment to discuss it between themselves. Happily, their answer was a resounding yes and within fifteen minutes we were on our way to the peace and comfort of my sitting room where we were soon installed in front of a cheery log fire with candles burning all around and a bit of Motown playing in the background. I have a long-standing obsession with vinyl records so will take any excuse to get the player cranked up and air a few tracks from my collection.

Being a Friday, I'd already offered them a bed for the night since none of us had any need to get up early the following day. This, of course, meant no-one had to worry about driving, which was fortunate since, after chatting and laughing our way through another hour or so, we'd worked our way almost to the bottom of our third bottles of wine. Thinking we'd better shift things up a gear before we simply drank ourselves into a triple coma, I suggested a dip in the ever-alluring hot tub. Liv, as it turned out, was still apparently feeling a little shy about getting naked so I offered to go first, stripping off completely to reveal evidence of my growing anticipation of the prospects ahead. She giggled a bit at first but it broke the ice very effectively and they both followed suit. We were soon outside, lowering ourselves into the hot tub where any remaining inhibitions rapidly retreated. In fact, Liv was completely transformed in that respect, becoming much more forthright and making it obvious she wanted to get physically acquainted as a matter of urgency. Gliding over towards me, she guided my hand down between her thighs where, I found, she was lusciously slippery and not just from the water in the tub. I continued to fondle her gently as she hovered in the water, nipples occasionally just breaking the

127

surface as she breathed deeply, her eyes closed. Keeping half an eye on Will, aware this was the first time he's have seen anyone else playing with his wife, I allowed my other hand to drift up to those tantalisingly inviting breasts. Without any further preamble or warning, she suddenly flicked open her eyes, came up close to my face and said, almost fiercely, 'I want you to fuck me, Dave, I want you to fuck me right now...'

Brilliant!

Keeping my gaze fixed on her deep, chocolate brown eyes, I half stood, sliding one arm around her waist so I could twist her through the water and switch places with her. This move accomplished, I could then wedge my feet against the angle between the base and the opposite side, which, experience told me, would give me the best grip. I let my free arm rest on the ledge behind her head, leaning my weight slightly against her chest to pin her into position. Tightening the arm around her waist to raise her off the seat where she'd landed, I lifted her hips to the perfect angle at which I could give her the urgent attention she'd requested. She arched up in unison, lined up to perfection so that with barely a thrust I slid easily inside her. She threw her head back, curls springing out in all directions, and gasped, pushing harder and harder up against me. I sensed movement from Will's side of the tub and momentarily flicked my radar in his direction in case a situation was developing but I needn't have worried, he was simply moving closer so he could caress Liv's face and hair and she nuzzled his hand in response.

It was autumn and there was already a chill in the air so I knew that exposed skin out above the water was going to get uncomfortably cold pretty quickly which slightly limited our options for variety so, before she really got into her stride, I gently broached the idea that we head back indoors where it was warmer. There seemed to an agreement that this was a sound plan so, grabbing towels as we went, we headed back to the house, laughing and giggling like naughty children. Rubbing each other down to stop the shivering, we grabbed another bottle of wine on our way through the kitchen. Will poured drinks and then settled back on the sofa in the sitting room while I got Liv on the floor in front of the fire. She looked adorably sexy laying there, hair spread out around her, eyes glinting in the firelight. I ran my hands lightly along the length of her smooth, firm body, lingering a while over her curves and contours before laying down on her, slowly beginning to move inside her once more while Will watched from the sofa. She was moaning contentedly, body yielding and rocking to the rhythm of my movements. I started to build pace a little, Liv simply submitting to the moment, seeming far away in a sensory world of her own, but as my sense of urgency began to increase she opened her eyes and gave me a faraway smile before her eyes drifted shut again, creasing slightly at the edges as her face gave away her approaching orgasm.

Glancing over towards Will, I made a silent enquiry, using the internationally recognised code of the sideways nod combined with single raised eyebrow, as to whether he wanted to get more involved at this point. He grinned and immediately left his lookout position on the sofa, coming forward to kneel beside his wife on the floor, stroking her hair and smiling at her as their eyes met. She reached over and grabbed his hand (I've often noticed this sort of thing happening in these threesome situations, particularly where the couple involved are obviously genuinely close) and as if, perhaps, permission had somehow been granted, she gave a long, shuddering exhale and succumbed to an almighty orgasm, almost squeezing me over the edge as she went.

While still in the final throes, she reached over to Will, taking his cock in her hand and drawing him towards her mouth. I withdrew, intending to let him have her to himself but as I eased away she reached down and grabbed me with her other hand, making it pretty clear she wanted us both involved. I checked again to see what was happening with Will. He was crouched over Liv, dick in her mouth, eyes closed, oblivious. Liv's grip on me was strong enough that it would have felt almost rude to pull away so I stayed put while she worked steadily away at me although with varying degrees of speed and focus as she still had a mouth and handful of Will to contend with at the same time. Given all of that, I thought she was doing an extremely creditable job for a novice. After a little while, her efforts had brought Will to the brink and shortly afterwards to climax, coming into her mouth and over her chin whilst she, after the briefest of pauses continued to work at me with steadfast intent until she triggered the inevitable explosion.

Will and I sat on either side of the smiling Liv while she, rather self-consciously, confessed that this had been one of the things that had revved up her interest in having a threesome in the first place. The juice of two men mixed on her body at the same time. It did occur to me to think that it might have been better if she'd mentioned that earlier. But, no matter, she was obviously happy with how things had panned out. Will seemed happy too and I was feeling very satisfied, so it had all worked out perfectly. By now it was about two o'clock in the morning so we all went to bed, Liv sleeping with Will in the spare room while I slept alone, although I'd (only half-jokingly) told them they could feel free to come wake me up for another instalment should they feel inclined at any time during the night. In the morning I sent them on their way with a cooked breakfast, which we ate sat round the table like old friends, no awkwardness at all. I think they left my house a very contented couple.

As it turned out, we were to meet up again a few weeks later although, this time, Will had organised our meeting at their house as a surprise for Liv. It was a Thursday night and she had been out at an evening class when I arrived. I must admit, she looked surprised but really pleased to see me there when she got back, scampering off upstairs, to change into something she considered more appropriate, namely a short denim skirt and loose, silky top, not that she was wearing them for very long as, between Will and myself, we had her naked again pretty quickly. While waiting for Liv to get home, Will and I had sat together with a beer and discussed a few things, during which time we'd agreed to start by spit roasting her. Liv, of course, had no idea what we'd planned but went very happily along with us undressing her in stages, me removing her top and bra then exploring her breasts with my mouth while my hands unbuttoned my own shirt and jeans, stripping them off as far as I could without interrupting my attention to her too much. Meanwhile, Will had unzipped and dropped her skirt, leaving her standing in just her panties and heels, looking very inviting, the mass of dark hair tumbling about her face bringing back the still recent memories of our previous session. Will knelt in front of her, easing the remaining underwear slowly down to the ground as he kissed and teased her pussy, warming her up for what was to come. Pushing back her glorious hair, I traced the length of her neck with my lips before sliding my tongue back down to her breasts. Will stood and guided Liv over to their sofa, getting her on all fours so he could kneel between her legs and take her from behind. Obviously, she realised straight away what we were up to and responded with a naughty grin before firmly guiding me towards her smiling lips as I stood at the end of the sofa, perfectly lined up to slide into her welcoming mouth.

Liv was in her element, plainly ecstatic to have this scenario sprung upon her and evidently keen to enjoy every minute. Her hands were running up and down as much of my body as she could reach, her tongue and lips enthusiastic and attentive. As the excitement gripped her, gasps and moans escaped from her already occupied mouth. It was a fantastic experience, especially with these two people whom I liked so much and felt so relaxed with. It was obvious that Liv did not want to shift positions at all, which was absolutely fine with me. Will had made half a move to change at one point but she hung on doggedly and he left well alone. I don't think he had any problem with it himself, just wanted to make sure she was alright. Plainly, she was. So, we continued as we were, all gradually becoming more lost in the moment, absorbed in the heat, skin, touch, sound and view of fantastic, unstoppable sex. I desperately didn't want it to be over too soon so, with grim determination, hung on as long as I possibly could, hoping they would too. Perhaps we were all thinking the same thing because, as it turned out we, by some miracle, all came more or less together. Fucking perfection!

I haven't got together with them again since but we still message occasionally and the option is potentially there to meet up at some point in the future. It was fantastic spending time with Liv and Will, although I have to say that, on balance, the vast majority of my experiences have proved to be positive. I have met some incredibly interesting and likeable people. The adage 'Everyone has their story' is true across the board and I've found it fascinating to discover some of the myriad reasons why people have become involved with this scene. Such a vast spectrum of circumstances, attitudes and experience out there. Everyone brings something different to the table, and the bed!

Let Me Sex You Up

Adam and Julia were a couple from the westernmost end of Kent who got in touch saying they were looking for a guy mostly just to play with Julia on her own while Adam watched, possibly with a little interaction from him if he felt like it. Their profile seemed fairly standard, more straight-forward than average perhaps but it all sounded fine to me so I responded and we began conversing. The initial exchanges were just between myself and Adam as he, apparently, set up and checked out all their encounters, but in the week before we met I was also exchanging messages with Julia so I was reassured that she was happy about it all and a willing particip-ant. It was a ninety minute drive to get to their place so I didn't arrive until around nine thirty for what was essentially a blind meet. I had a pretty good idea of what to expect but hadn't seen much in the way of photos so I felt a touch of trepidation as I approached their house and rang the bell.

Adam threw the door wide and welcomed me in, rapidly set-ting me up with a beer and doing his best to make me feel right at home. He was about the same height as me, dark haired and I would hazard a guess that he would fall into the general category of good looking from a woman's point of view. He called up the stairs to Julia who said she was on her way down shortly so Adam and I sat on their large, comfy sofa, chatting, while we waited for Julia to join us. I was feel-ing pretty relaxed by the time she appeared, making her en-trance after I'd been there for around ten minutes and prov-ing herself to be well up there on the spectrum of womanly attractiveness. So far, so good, everything was shaping up well and I was glad I'd taken a chance on this particular blind date. Introductions made, the three of us then sat and chat-

133

ted for another twenty minutes or so while she caught up with a drink before we all agreed it was time to start moving things along, refreshing glasses and heading off upstairs. With her blonde hair, wide brown eyes and spectacular cheekbones, Julia had been having no difficulty whatsoever in holding my attention. The more I looked at her the more I was thinking 'Jackpot!' She was gorgeous but also had a cheeky wit and contagious laugh which made her a pretty good package all round. I was looking forward to getting things started.

If it seems at this stage a little improbable to you that I have found so many attractive women on my swinging travels, I promise I'm not just being nice (or delusional!). It would be fair to say there are a number of people on this scene who are perhaps there because they struggle for a date for one reason or another but most are there simply because this brand of sexual activity appeals to them and is something they want to be involved with. It's just a preference and those preferences may be held by anybody at all, with no automatic reference to their looks necessarily. Certainly, with one or two notable exceptions, on the whole I've been pleasantly surprised more often than I've been disappointed by the appearance of the women I've met while doing this. I suspect Julia had made an effort with her appearance but she was, in fact, naturally beautiful so perhaps hadn't had to work too hard at it. I was slightly surprised that she'd chosen to wear quite a long, flowing dress; it was nice enough but seemed like an odd choice, although she could have worn a sack and still been attractive regardless. However, her motive became apparent when we got to the bedroom. Slipping the top section down over her breasts, the whole thing dropped straight to the floor leaving her standing there stark naked in a nanosecond. It was a nice trick. 'Bravo!' I thought, all but giving her a round of applause.

She had a superb figure and was not at all shy about showing it off, obviously enjoying being openly admired and the focus of our attention. I was starting to respond to this inviting sight already and, since it seemed rude to leave her standing there naked all alone, I began easing myself out of my clothes too. She encouraged me while she watched me with apparent interest, the slightest flicker of an eyebrow indicating her appreciation of my unashamedly eager appendage when he made his appearance. Smiling, she came towards me and then, without taking her eyes off mine, reached down, grabbed me by the dick and led me over to the bed. I didn't have much choice but to follow her there, not that I had any inclination whatsoever to resist. She sat on the edge of the bed, pulling me towards her as she did so and then proceeded to stroke and encourage me to complete fullness. He didn't need a whole lot of coaxing, but she took her time and seemed to be taking great pleasure in admiring me, something which is almost guaranteed to have a positive effect on any man. Once she was happy that her work was progressing well, she carefully and deliberately drew back my foreskin and ran her tongue around the end before taking me into her mouth and, using her hands, lips and tongue to great effect, brought me to the brink within minutes. It was impossible to resist this vision, this naked, blonde goddess. I sincerely hoped it wasn't all going to be over too quickly but the sight of her working on me made my head spin with ecstasy and closing my eyes just made it worse as my mind skittered off in all directions. Fortunately, skilled as she was, every time she felt me getting to the edge she would stop for a moment before resuming, delicately licking me with the tip of her tongue and starting up again when I was back under control. Damn, she was good. So good. And so damned beautiful. I don't think there have been many I've encountered who have been able to get me to that point so incredibly fast and been able to balance it for so long. It was a masterclass, she should definitely give lessons.

Just when I was starting to wonder how much more of this sweet, sweet torture I could take, she released me and lay back on the bed, opening her legs so I had a good view and gently playing with herself, her slippery fingers showing me plainly just how ready she was. I let her continue for a few minutes, drinking in the sight of this amazingly gorgeous woman performing for my benefit, before I lowered myself between her legs, drawing myself through her juices, gently back and forth until we were both glistening with them.

Meanwhile, Adam was moving around the bed, watching what was going on and starting to add the odd word of instruction or encouragement. Not intrusively and I wasn't getting any bad vibe there so I just went along with it. Julia, by now, was making some quite encouraging noises of her own so I began to push my way through her juicy lips while she teased and pinched her own nipples until they were standing up like little pink flagpoles. Just an inch. Withdrew. An inch and a half. Withdrew. Now she was really starting to make some noise, her frustrated anticipation apparent. In and out, a little deeper each time, until she cried out, virtually shouting 'Oh my god, I can't take it, go in hard, this is killing me...' Being a gentleman, of course I obliged, forcing my way in to full depth in one thrust and coming fully out again before plunging full in again and thereafter pummelling her as hard as I could while Adam chipped in with "that's great, she's taken all of your cock now mate", as if, perhaps, I hadn't quite noticed or something. "She'll come soon" he added, which, again, I think I could have worked out for myself. He was absolutely right though. Almost immediately, she began to shudder beneath me and I felt her legs come up and wrap around my back as she gave way to her climax, moaning, her muscles contracting hard on me, the extra friction bringing me off too, squeezing out every last drop I had to offer.

I stayed put while she rode the last of it, her eyes eventually flickering open and making contact again. I withdrew once she'd released her grip on my neck and unwrapped her legs, half contemplating turning her over and, as I was still pretty hard, seeing if I could have her from behind while we were at it. But, sadly, she looked like she was done and the ever-present Adam was there to point out that, as it was now past midnight, perhaps that was enough for one session. I suppose he had a point and I did have a pretty long drive home ahead of me. They offered to have me stay over the rest of the night and I must admit I was tempted as I was pretty knackered and I suppose there might have been the potential for another session in the morning, but, as usual, that post-coital sense of mild euphoria had descended on me and I opted to drive back with a happy heart and a satisfied smile on my face, taking mental snapshots of the vision of Julia in various positions as I drove.

I messaged them afterwards to thank them and we exchanged a few more emails. I'd have loved to play with Julia again but given that it was a three hour plus round trip to get to them I didn't pursue them too hard, although I did leave them with an open invitation to come and visit me if they ever fancied it.

David B

Tiny Tina

I saw Tina's profile on the website I've had the most success with overall and liked the look of her immediately as her profile was quite cleverly written, which appealed, even though she'd only posted a single body shot in the photo section. She is married and her husband has no idea that she is registered on this site or even that she is remotely interested in this kind of encounter. She told me that they had been married a long time and the marriage had proved somewhat lacking in love as well as being, in her opinion, an abject failure in the bedroom too. Since they both travelled with work she occasionally had an opportunity to indulge in her own independent sex-life while her husband remained oblivious. It did cross my mind to wonder if he was, perhaps, of a similar opinion and out doing the same thing and how amusing it would be if they spotted one another on their respective sites.

She lived quite a distance away but was up for a meet and we eventually managed to coordinate an evening meet, arranging to get together for a preliminary drink at a bar in St Albans. Quite a long drive for me but I there wasn't a great deal else going on at the time and I had a positive vibe about the idea of meeting her. Oddly, I was really attracted by the emails she'd written, I had a feeling she was going to be an interesting girl. I was right, she was very lively and very funny, full of witty quips and amusing stories. We were chatting animatedly and laughing our heads off in no time at all. She was also absolutely tiny. Such a lovely, frisky, teeny-weeny package. She'd listed herself as size 6 so I wasn't expecting someone oversized but she really was petite, although perfectly proportioned and very attractive with it. I was quite mesmerised by this miniature person and almost immediately found myself wondering what her minute hands would feel like wrapped around my dick. I just couldn't help it.

The evening seemed to go really well, with drinks evolving into dinner at Jamie Oliver's in St Albans and the conversation flowing easily throughout the evening. She was obviously a pretty sharp cookie, successful in her work and an absolute comedian with many an anecdote to share. She kept me thoroughly entertained. Whether we were laughing or talking a little too loudly or whether, perhaps, it was just obvious from the body language between us, the waiting staff had plainly got the gist of what was happening by the time we left and we had a few knowing looks as we made our way out of the restaurant. I even had a wink from one of them. Feeling a bit conspicuous but not really caring much by then we drifted outside and I escorted Tina back to her car. Sadly, especially as it had been such a long drive there to meet her, she had to go home that night and we reluctantly parted with promises of another, full on get together some time soon.

I am disappointed to report that, although we exchanged messages for a while afterwards, we haven't made that second meet happen as yet and I suppose this one might have to be filed in the list of 'entertaining evenings' only. It was great meeting her and I enjoyed her company immensely but I'd have liked to get my hands on her uniquely gorgeous little body .

David B

I Don't Get a Kick Out of You

In complete contrast to my rendezvous with Tiny Tina, I had a rather less entertaining preliminary meet on Monday evening of the following week at the Red Lion in Storrington. It was with a couple, Phil and Shona, who had only put up a profile a few days earlier. We'd made fairly rapid progress as I'd sent them a message as soon as I saw their profile and I'd had a reply back pretty quickly with a few photos. Perhaps I should have read the warning signs when there were just body shots of Shona, none of her face, and none of Phil at all, even when we were privately exchanging pictures. But, despite previous lessons and experience, I didn't really question it, I just assumed they wanted to keep their privacy which, especially since they were newbies, would have seemed normal and understandable. I could see that Shona had a great body anyway so I continued the exchange agreed to meet up with them, putting their enthusiasm down to being new to the scene and keen to get things moving.

I made my way over to Storrington, arriving earlier than our agreed time, found a table with a good view of the entrance and got myself a drink while I waited for them to arrive. I was slightly taken by surprise when they almost immediately appeared at my side and introduced themselves. They were, by all accounts, already there when I'd arrived but it was just as well they'd recognised me as I would have had great difficulty picking them out. Even though I'd seen no head-shots, I'd felt I had enough information to go on but would never have recognised them from their profile descriptions. Nothing like the slim attractive couple I was expecting, in fact, quite the opposite. Phil was short, fat and wearing shorts. On a cold, rainy evening in late October! It just seemed a bit odd. Shona was slim and looked like she might indeed have had a decent body hidden under her slouchy clothes but, to my eyes, she was exceedingly unattractive. And that was being kind. No wonder she hadn't provided any face shots. Deciding to give them a chance to grow on me, and myself a chance to finish my drink, I stayed and chatted with them for about forty-five minutes. During this time, sadly, my opinion got worse rather than better. I found Phil very brash and overbearing whilst Shona seemed particularly vacuous and barely able to contribute to the conversation. I discovered that this was the fourth time they'd set up a profile on that particular website. Four different profiles over an eight month period. There was something a bit odd about that too and I didn't feel inclined to stick around to find out what.

So, it was a bit of a waste of an evening but if you put yourself out there I guess you've got to expect to meet all sorts on your travels. Even with a bit of experience behind you it is unlikely that every encounter you instigate or follow up will lead to a positive outcome and it would be wrong of me to suggest that this was the case. Suffice to say that I did not meet up with them again, even though they messaged me several times afterwards to request another meet. That surprised me as I was pretty sure I had let it be known that I didn't want to take things any further. Perhaps I should have made my feelings clearer on the night but that old issue with not wanting to upset people or be mean had kicked in again. They even asked me to provide a verification for them, cheeky buggers.

The profile of theirs that I'd see then disappeared but I see they have now posted a new one under the same username so I will be giving that a miss.

David B

Maria

Sometimes, when there have been a couple of disappointing meets in a row, it can all seem a bit too much like hard work. But, then, along will come the simplest and most fantastic experience to remind me exactly why I do this. I'd been chatting from time to time with a couple from a village not too far away, Stuart and Maria, over the course of several weeks. It was a slow-burner but we seemed to be getting on pretty well and I must admit I was impressed enough with the photos I'd seen of Maria to keep me interested in pursuing it. Happening to exchange a couple of messages at the start of one particular weekend, we realised that none of us had plans for the Saturday evening and spontaneously decided to meet up and see what transpired, convening early in the evening for a few drinks at The Robin Hood pub in Rowlands Castle.

Stuart was stockily built but very well dressed, well groomed and well spoken. Everything about him immediately gave the impression of wealth, not least his extremely hot and immaculately presented wife. Tall, blonde, blue-eyed and long-legged, Maria had it all going on and attracted a fair few admiring glances as she crossed the bar. From our email conversations, I was aware that they dabbled in swinging as Stuart was impotent so the occasional introduction of an additional partner opened up their options a bit. I guess sometimes you just can't have it all. It must have been incredibly frustrating to be married to a divinely beautiful woman like Maria and not be physically able to make the absolute most of it. Her manner was, perhaps, a little cool to start with but she warmed up fairly quickly, perhaps just wanting her husband to take the lead initially. She was very pleasingly attired in a short skirt, black boots and a blouse that was slightly too small in that gorgeous way which serves to make a well blessed woman's upper anatomy even more eye-catching than it already is. Said blouse was undone just enough to give me glimpses of the enticingly lacy-edged bra beneath and a most inspiring cleavage view whenever she leaned forward to take her drink from the table. Her restrained breasts seemed to be positively begging for release, but perhaps that was just wishful thinking on my part.

I came to the conclusion that, although they had a bit of history with swinging, they didn't organise meets very often. Quite honestly, judging by how long it had taken us to get to this point, I can't say I'm surprised since many potential partners would probably have gone off the boil long before this pair were ready to take things forward. It was such a genial meet that I was lulled by the general ambiance, perfectly content to sit there for quite a while, sipping wine and surveying the tantalising landscape before me as the conversation flowed along. Within a very short space of time, they felt almost like old friends. Funny how that happens sometimes. It was fortunate, too, because I sensed that rushing forward was not something these two were about and I had the distinct feeling that any attempt to push things along would be rebuffed and most likely derail the whole process there and then. So we comfortably whiled away an hour or so before deciding to have dinner there together too. It felt like a perfectly natural and pleasant way to spend an evening. I was quite happy really and had all but dismissed the idea of anything more occurring that night so just relaxed into enjoying their company for the moment. Eventually, returning from a visit to the men's room, I discovered that they had taken the opportunity to discuss the situation and decided that they would very much like to take things to the next level right away. They both seemed enthusiastic, excitedly encouraging me to come back with them to their home as soon as we had finished our meal. This was a very welcome turn of events, not least since by this time I had become exceedingly attached to the idea of liberating Maria's poor constricted breasts from their lacy confinement. So, I agreed without hesitation. I gave them the option of coming back to my house but they seemed to prefer the idea of their own home and we headed off there, in convoy, a short while later.

The conversation had become a little more flirtatious once this decision had been made, although still at a lesser rate than most meets would have done, but they seemed pretty fired up by the time we arrived at their beautiful and imposing house. While Stuart fetched glasses and wine from the kitchen, things were moving along nicely in the sitting room, soon giving me the opportunity to get my hands on Maria's delectable breasts whilst she appeared equally intent on getting my own credentials out in full view. My readiness for action was plainly apparent, which appeared to please her greatly. I was obliged to pause while she sank down and continued her explorations with her mouth. Meanwhile, Stuart had reappeared, setting the glasses carefully down on the coffee table before casually removing his trousers and taking up position in an armchair which would give him a good view of the action. As he watched our progress, he seemed very engaged with what was going on and was openly giving himself plenty of stimulation but he didn't appear to be having any success in becoming erect. I wondered briefly when the last time had been that they'd had sex but was quickly brought back to the present by Maria's increasingly vigorous attentions. I leaned back on the sofa while she busied herself in my lap, torn between the almost torturous pleasure she was giving me and the overwhelming desire to reacquaint myself with those wonderful breasts. A tantalising choice.

The breasts won.

I gently eased her up to the appropriate level, relishing the sight of her enormously erect nipples before thoroughly tending to each one in turn. Stuart was emitting sounds of enjoyment too, obviously getting at least some erotic pleasure from the scene being played out before him. Unlike the scenario with Maggie and Tom, these two seemed completely comfortable with the whole set up, both happy to allow one another their own enjoyment and seeming very together. Evidently a couple that these kind of arrangements actually worked well for. Needless to say, I was more than happy to be of service Leaning intently in towards me, Maria fixed me with her clear blue eyes and said that she needed to take me upstairs, then she rose and pulled me up off the sofa, without waiting for a response. I didn't mind anyway. To be honest I think I'd have unquestioningly followed those breasts wherever they wanted to take me. 'Coming?' she said to Stuart. I don't think she realised she'd just said something a bit close to the mark but, fortunately, Stuart didn't appear to register it either, getting to his feet with an accommodating smile as we all headed up to the bedroom.

Sitting me on the edge of the bed, Maria began to undress, slowly and seductively, smiling and moving as she did. It was a wondrous thing to watch, especially when she finally discarded the bra fully, revealing the focal point of my adoration in all their glory. She had a deliciously magnificent body - toned, pert, buffed and polished. My heart momentarily went out to Stuart and his incapacity, although I'm sure they had found plenty of other ways to satisfy one another over the years as there was an undeniable physical closeness between them.

Determined to make every effort to be a satisfactory substitute, I set about pleasuring Maria in as many ways as I could think of while Stuart looked on, seemingly with great satisfaction, although still not so much as a twitch from his lad despite his constant manual encouragement. Perhaps because she didn't get to engage in full sex terribly often, Maria embraced the variety, throwing herself wholeheartedly into enjoying each position I put forward and adding a few ideas of

145

her own until it seemed we had exhausted most options. Finally, with her perfectly curved arse perched on the edge of her dressing table (delectably reflected in triplicate in the mirrors behind) and her toned thighs hitched round my waist, she had come to her noisy, heaving climax, at last allowing me to open my own floodgates with equal vigour.

Still breathing heavily, I disentangled myself from Maria's endless legs then helped her ease herself off the dressing table, a slightly amused grin passing between us at the sudden incongruity. As I collapsed back on to the bed, she drifted over to sit with Stuart, draping herself across him and snuggling into his chest. Drawing her to him and kissing the top of her head, he closed his eyes and they sat together looking very cosy and contented for a few minutes before Stuart politely asked if I'd like coffee.

While he went off to the kitchen to make a pot, Maria became aware that I was still almost fully hard. She gave me a surprised look and quite honestly I was pretty surprised myself after the battering he just been subjected to. Her face melted into a slightly disbelieving smile when I explained, I don't think she was immediately convinced, but by the time Stuart had returned with the coffee I had Maria on the bed, her legs hard back against her shoulders while I pummelled her for a second time. Not too surprisingly, a rather shorter and less creative session, after our recent antics. Fortunately, I built very quickly to a point of release and, not sure how much more action I was going to be able to take in all honesty, I seized the moment and withdrew, unloading irresistibly over those gloriously luscious breasts, a fitting finale to such an exuberantly sex-packed evening. Hoping I hadn't cut short her pleasure too much, I shot her a slightly apologetic glance but she met my eyes with a smile and we lay there side by side for a few moments while Stuart poured the coffee.

We all stayed and relaxed in the bedroom for a while, chatting amiably over our coffee before I decided it was time to head home. Such lovely people, I had thoroughly enjoyed getting to know them as well as having had a sensational evening. We still keep in touch from time to time and I'd love to think we might meet up again at some point.

David B

Penny For Your Thoughts

For me, Christmas is always a difficult time, still rather tinged with sadness and emotionally a bit of a challenge. Seeing everyone else being caught up in their happiness and excitement simply serves to make me feel more keenly my ongoing sense of loss and it can be a depressing and unforgiving time. However, there are many, many people out there who also find it difficult for a million different reasons and it can sometimes help shine a light into your own dark corners when you have an insight into other people's situations and to know you are not the only person suffering. It makes it feel, perhaps, a little less personal and can help you rise above your own circumstances. In early December, I had an encounter which did exactly that for me.

A new profile appeared on one of the sites in late November. It had very little information and no photos so it was not the most obvious of additions and would have been very easy to skip over. It also had no verifications but I dropped in anyway to have a look and something about it made me pause. After a little consideration I tentatively sent off a short message. It was a few days before I heard back but when I did it all became clear. The profile had been posted by a woman, Penny, whose husband was serving an overseas posting with the military and who wasn't going to be home for Christmas, if he came home at all. It was plain from her reply that she was very anxious about the possibility of him never making it back here, not least since a number of his fellow servicemen had been flown home in boxes in recent months having fallen in the line of duty.

Penny and her husband had been occasionally active on the swinging scene over the previous few years, so they knew what was involved and how it worked which had led them to hit on an idea to help overcome the anguish and frustration of his absence. So, Penny had the slightly unusual request of an encounter at her house which would be conducted with a live interactive video connection to her husband throughout. Quite honestly, I thought this was genius and lost no time in responding to her slightly tentative request with a very positive response and offering full co-operation if she wanted to take things further. Happily for me, she did. As things were constantly changing in the war-zone in which her husband was serving, she was keen to set up a meet as soon as possible to take advantage of his current free access to the necessary online facilities, not knowing when that availability might change. It was, therefore, just a couple of days later that we met briefly for coffee to make sure we were both happy to go ahead. I was half expecting she might want to have her husband tuned in for that part too but apparently that wasn't necessary. She was casually dressed, dark haired with pretty blue eyes and a slim, taut and wirily athletic body. Despite seeming slightly anxious on first appearance, we chatted fairly easily, making that polite sort of conversation that you do when in a public place, don't know one another very well and are trying not to be too conspicuous or say anything that might get people's ears twitching. We managed that quite successfully although still sharing occasional, mutually knowing smiles, which spoke volumes. She had taken a half hour break from work to get to our meet so it was over very quickly but was, fortunately, enough to persuade her that I would be suitable. Given the urgency of the situation, we made a date there and then and just a few days later I headed over to her house for this slightly unorthodox meet.

When I arrived, fairly early in the evening, Penny seemed slightly tense although this turned out to be more to do with technology connections than anything else. She handed me a drink when I arrived then perched on the arm of the sofa and made an attempt at conversation while we waited for the allotted time to arrive. After a little while, she took me upstairs and showed me the bedroom, where she already had everything set up, laptop positioned at an angle from which the bed was clearly visible. We talked through what she was planning at which point she asked me, very politely, if I would mind keeping sounds and talking to a minimum once the connection was up and running as this was meant to be therapy for him too and she wanted to make sure that what he was getting was going to be mostly visual and focused on 'her', rather than 'us'. It seemed a reasonable request and it wasn't any problem for me so I just told her to tell me what she wanted once we were underway and I'd just shut up and get on with the job. That made her laugh and seemed to break the tension a little. I wasn't feeling any great concerns myself but it was probably the most pressure to perform on demand that I'd felt to date and I was glad I now had quite a few of these kinds of situations under my belt for experience before this one cropped up. I took the opportunity to ask her about her husband but got not a great deal of information, just an overwhelming impression of her passion for him and her anguish at his absence, something I could relate to in my own situation.

Penny was wearing a soft jersey dress, pointed out that it would lift easily up over her head when the time came. It's always useful to know that sort of thing in advance and I inwardly commended her for her forethought. She suggested that, when the call came through, I should go into the bathroom and get undressed while she had a brief chat with her husband and she would let me know when she was ready to get started. She then asked me how I was feeling and whether I needed a little 'stimulation' to get me going. I wasn't quite sure what she meant. Was she suddenly going to produce Viagra for me, perhaps? I reassured her that I was just fine and would make sure I was ready for action, before remembering my manners and asking her if she was in need of any stimulation herself. Something in the way I asked must have struck her as amusing as she fell about in fits of giggles. Or perhaps it was nerves. In any case, once she'd composed herself she said she thought she would be fine and that the idea of seeing her husband and then him watching her having sex was already having the desired effect on her. Regardless of this exchange, she did come forward and gave me a friendly rub, just a gentle one, and if she couldn't tell beforehand that I was looking forward to our imminent session then I strongly suspect that she could by the time she'd finished. She withdrew her hand and smiled sweetly at me but with slightly raised eyebrows which gave her a rather naughty and very inviting expression. Nope, getting it up for her wasn't going to be any problem at all.

With that, the laptop sounded its ringtone and I slipped out to get undressed, leaving the door open and half listening to the exchange of voices, more to get a sense of his tone rather than any particular interest in what was being said. It had occurred to me that I knew nothing of this man really and was taking Penny's word for it that he was expecting this show to happen. I hoped that all was as it seemed and had my radar on half alert for warning signs. He had a gruff voice but sounded good humoured enough and there was an easy banter going on between them right away. Phew, it sounded like it was all going to be fine. I stood, naked, in the bathroom doorway, waiting for my moment, suddenly stifling a half-laugh as it crossed my mind that it was a bit like waiting to go stage for Britain's Got Talent or something similar, preparing to perform my party piece in front of a TV audience. The thought had me grinning away to myself as I waited to be called in from the wings.

I set about teasing the beast into fully aroused status, figuring I'd better be ready for battle when the moment came. I heard Penny say that I was ready and her husband's reply of 'great,

151

let's get the party started'! She turned to me and smiled, giving me a second wry smile when she saw that I was, indeed, ready to party. I went forward into the bedroom and she said into the camera 'Alan, this is Dave'.

'Hi Dave, you lucky bastard!' he, laughingly, replied, 'you better be good to my girl.'

'I'll certainly do my best' I assured him, 'she's a fine girl you've got here'.

We exchanged one or two more comments and he then addressed Penny direct and said 'come on then, get that dress off, woman. Let's see you'. I stood back while she lifted the dress off and threw it onto the chair, turning and posing for him in her underwear while Alan made appreciative sounds and encouraging comments. She blew him kisses then turned and wiggled her bum at him, tantalisingly pulling the underwear down over one cheek. Any remaining tension was immediately erased. In this guise she was a very attractive woman and her sexy teasing was done in a fun way but with a slinky confidence, quite the little kitten. Frankly, I'm surprised a sex-starved man in a distant land needed much more than Penny could have shown him by herself in just a few minutes to get him to breaking point, but he obviously wanted the full show and was asking for my input pretty soon.

'Get her kit off then, Dave', he offered, and I stepped straight in to oblige, turning her towards the screen while I stood behind her, slipping her straps over her shoulders before unclasping and dropping her pretty coverings, revealing her fully to the obviously attentive Alan. Slowly, I slid my hands round to massage her freshly liberated breasts until her nipples were standing proud. Sliding my hands backwards and up, I lifted her arms above her head before returning to her breasts and continuing to stroke and caress them. It was tempting to keep checking the screen to see what reaction this was getting from Alan but I could unquestionably hear that this was positive so thought it best to keep my eyes averted and focus on Penny, leaving him to watch in peace. She half turned so that she was side on to the camera, bringing my face down to her chest so I could lick and suck in Alan's full view. Taking advantage of the opportunity, I began to ease off the rest of her underwear, slowly down, further and further until it simply dropped to the floor. I suppose it could be said that one of the advantages of the less curvy female is that their clothes do seem to come off more easily. Not that wrestling undergarments off a more generously proportioned lady isn't every bit as much fun, but for the purposes of this session, Penny's more athletic shape worked particularly well.

Still orally attached to Penny's delectable nipples, I turned her again towards the screen, moving slightly to the side so that Alan could watch as I stroked my way down the outside of Penny's thigh then up between her legs, cupping her in my hand and sliding my middle finger deeper to see how she was coming along. It appeared she was coming along very nicely, in fact as I slid my hand gently back and forth I felt her tense and gasp, making me wonder if she was going to come there and then, which, of course, wouldn't have done at all. Hurriedly, withdrawing my hand, I stood up and guided her gently backwards until she was sitting on the edge of the bed. Standing to the side of her, I pushed her legs further apart and let my hand drift back down. She leaned back slightly, resting on her elbows but kept her head up so she could keep some kind of eye contact with the screen while I fingered her with one hand, the other teasing her breasts.

'Go down on her, Dave', came Alan's voice across the ether. He sounded gruffer than ever and very much like a man who was struggling to contain himself. I knelt between Penny's legs, trying to give Alan as good a view as possible, and buried my tongue in her crevice, feeling her drop back onto the bed. She shuffled back and spread her legs wide, anchoring her feet on the edge of the bed and lifting her hips. I wrapped my arms round the tops of her legs and buried my face between them. I hoped Alan was getting everything he wanted or needed from this because I was certainly enjoying my part in the show. Her strong, malleable body had me quite inflamed by this point and I would have found it extremely disappointing to have to stop now. I was doing my best to keep positioning us for Alan's maximum benefit but I am only human and the heat of the moment was making it difficult to stay focused on anything much other than the fact that I now desperately wanted to fuck Penny's brains out. Unable to fight off the urge any longer, I stood, keeping my arms under her legs, lifting and straightening them, turning her slightly to give a better view, in a last salute to Alan, before bringing her to meet me and sliding firmly inside her. Firm was the word, too, she was slippery but tight, the perfect combination, the sensation nearly brought me off straight away and I had to slow down to a gentle rhythm to avoid a too-early conclusion. Penny had her arms spread wide open, head pushed back, legs now wrapped round my back pulling me in deep but preventing me moving too much which was probably no bad thing for a minute or two while I got the overwhelming urges I'd been feeling back under control.

Transported to that sacred place where communication with earthly things is pretty much lost, I'd been gradually building the pace again for a while when Penny started to shift position beneath me, bringing me slightly back in touch with the here and now. Somewhere deep in the back of my brain, I finally finished processing some sounds which had emanated from the laptop behind me. Eventually, the words 'turn her over mate...' filtered through into cognition. Penny had obviously heard them straight away, hence her movement, and since the idea didn't seem a bad one at all, I complied, easing back as Penny rotated onto all fours before ploughing on once more. New but equally intense sensations in this position and, even in my slightly detached state, I could see that there must have been a visual benefit from Alan's viewpoint. He was speaking now and then but, of course, it was generally directly to Penny, hence my zoning out from what was actually being said. Occasionally he would suggest something which Penny, being rather more aware of his presence than I was, would pick up on and instigate while I would just do as I was directed and continue to enjoy the fun in whatever position had been offered. I found myself laying on my back with my legs over the side of the bed while Penny rode me in reverse cowboy, upright, facing the screen, obviously interacting with Alan whilst I reclined, enjoying the view from behind and the sensations below.

The tone of Alan's voice suggested that he was very absorbed in what he was seeing and that it was having a profound effect. Penny seemed to be mostly responding in moans and sighs with the occasional few words thrown in. Fortunately, our triangular situation appeared to be building to crescendo at roughly the same pace on all sides, certainly I was feeling my own tension starting to mount and was now fighting to keep it locked down as long as possible. It seemed to me that Penny was nearing the brink too so it was something of a relief when I heard sounds from the screen which seemed to indicate that Alan had got there first. Penny, still astride me and facing Alan was quick to follow so I seized the moment, and her hips, keeping her moving with enough friction to bring about my release too. For a minute or so there was little but the sound of intense breathing as we all drifted along in the aftermath. I lay still under the weight of the now-spent Penny, enjoying those moments until the husky voice of Alan began to come through over the airwaves once again, causing her to ease herself off me and move over to plant herself on the stool in front of the screen, where they continued to converse in low voices. Leaving them to their private time, I headed off back to the bathroom where I quickly hopped into the shower before dressing.

When I ventured back to the bedroom, the connection had been either closed or lost, Penny still sitting on the stool by the laptop, looking a little wistful. 'Everything ok?' I asked. She responded with a broad smile before saying that everything was great and that Alan had asked her to say 'bye' and 'thanks' from him but had had to sign off. It seemed he had been pretty happy with the way things had gone and they at least felt they'd had some sexual interaction, albeit remotely. Funny how it works for some people, I guess the fact that they'd dabbled in the swinging scene previously allowed them to carry this meet through without any issues. Due to the time difference we'd had to accommodate between his country and here, it was still quite early, so we chatted on for a little while and had another drink. She told me they'd met when they were very young and had clocked up nearly twenty years together. They'd been married for quite a few of those years but had been unable to have children, which made it even harder to bear the time apart when he was posted away as she felt the lack of his presence all the more keenly. At Christmas, particularly, despite a busy social and work life, this made her feel quite isolated and as they were coming towards the end of a fairly long stint apart on this occasion, she was weary of the waiting and the worrying.

Of course, a lot of what she was saying resonated with me and, although she would be, barring dire incidents, reunited with her partner in the next month or so, I felt a degree of empathy and was glad to have helped in some way. Obviously, I'd had quite bit of enjoyment in the 'helping' too so I couldn't honestly claim a saintly role for myself but it did give me additional pleasure and satisfaction to feel I'd contributed something to a difficult situation which was having positive repercussions for everyone.

Don't Be Lonely This Christmas

With my experience having put my own issues into perspective a little, I decided to take a different and more positive approach to the approaching season. While most people were rushing around like headless chickens, shopping for baubles and the like, my own personal baubles and I set about making the festive period on the swinging scene zing even more than usual. I was well into the culture of it by now and, most importantly, had an ever-growing number of positive verifications to my name, which was improving the number and quality of my connections immeasurably. This was resulting in me now being contacted by some of the more established site users and making the introductory phase generally shorter, leading to a much faster turnaround of meets. There was also a general improvement in the way meets played out as there seemed to be a lot less suspicion or hesitation. Making full use of this set of circumstances I set about creating my swinging version of the Twelve Days of Christmas with a concentrated selection of seasonal treats for myself.

The first was on the 6th of December. I met with a couple, Martin and Janine, with whom I'd exchanged just a few messages before being invited to meet at their house. Despite their photos consisting of body shots only, something which had proved negative on some previous occasions, the sheer number of verifications on their list led me to trust and go with their invitation. I was greeted at the front door by Martin, who invited me into the lounge where a most pleasing and enticing sight awaited me. The blonde and very lovely Janine was perched on the edge of the sofa, long, elegantly crossed legs in black boots, stockings visible just below the

157

edge of her skirt and black blouse open almost to the waist revealing glimpses of what promised to be a fabulously sexy figure which was exactly as it was portrayed in her stunning photographs, if not better. Moment of truth over, I could relax and, reluctantly peeling my eyes away from the vision on the sofa, cheerfully accept the wine Martin was offering me.

As they had indicated would happen in their emails, Martin took the lead with the scenarios and I just had to go along with what transpired. After a very brief chat, really no more than a few minutes, he suggested we start to play and whisked us straight up to the bedroom. He had me undress while he removed his own clothes and Janine's blouse and skirt, leaving her just in bra, panties, stockings and boots. She looked incredible, all endless legs and gleaming hair, and this was having a very obvious effect on us both.

She reached out and gently started to play with me, making appreciative sounds at which point Martin said 'Yes, alright, go on then.' Apparently this gave her permission to start on me with her mouth as she then turned and crawled onto the bed, giving me a wickedly naughty look that beckoned me forward to join her. I knelt before her on the covers, prickling with anticipation as she bent her head and began to traced lines with her tongue up and down my length. She repeated this quite a number of times, then stopped to blow gently, her breath leaving slightly chill patterns as it caught her tongue's trails. It was intensely sensual and had me almost bursting with eagerness before she finally slid her lips delicately over my tip and I felt the contrasting heat as she took me deep into her mouth. Martin, meanwhile, went and stood behind her, slipping her underwear down and using his hand on her, producing a brightly coloured dildo from somewhere a few minutes later to continue his work. Janine seemed to be enjoying this interplay, moaning between mouthfuls, while I could see from the glistening dildo that she was clearly responding to the attention. 'There you go, she's nice and wet for you mate' said Martin, eventually. Taking my cue from this remark, I switched places with him, getting into position between the shiny black lengths of Janine's kinky boots. I had to admit he was right as I slid inside her almost effortlessly, hands resting on her perfectly curved hips as I guided her back towards me. Smoothly working her back and forth, I lost myself in the bliss of her slippery depths while she feasted on Martin, her pleasure audibly evident. The view from my new position was pretty hot, Janine's fabulous and naughtily encased body moving in front of me, silky skin so inviting.

Things were unexpectedly about to get even more interesting though. Janine suddenly started to straighten up and some presumably pre-ordained communication passed between her and Martin. Although she hadn't uttered a word, he responded verbally to her and started to change position. My flow was interrupted momentarily when she pulled slowly away from me and laid across the bed. He rolled her onto her side and spooned in behind her and I was left wondering where things were headed for a moment, especially when Martin produced a tube of lube which, from my experience so far, Janine had no need of whatsoever. I soon realised what was going on, however, when he lubed himself up and started working his way in through the back door, as it were.

Light dawned and I was suddenly faced with asking myself the question of how I felt about getting into such close proximity with another guy. To be fair, Martin gave me the option to decline but in that situation, mid flow with a stunning woman in front of me with her legs akimbo, I admit I probably decided differently than I might have done if I'd asked myself the same question sitting in front of my laptop with a coffee in my hand. As it was, it didn't seem such a big deal and I decided to go for it, although I did throw in a 'never done this before' comment so they were aware I was a novice. It transpired later that they'd suspected that anyway and decided to take me unawares and see how things evolved rather than force the issue before we'd even got started. Martin withdrew and got me to lie on the bed with my legs hanging over the edge while Janine straddled me and got me back inside her. She then leaned forward to offer Martin a good point of entry although this also left her breasts skimming my chest, something which, naturally, gave me insane pleasure and at least partly distracted me from thinking too hard about what else was happening. Martin had eased in behind her and gently started to work his way back into her with the application of yet more lube. I kind of wished I'd had a couple more glasses of wine before getting into this, as I might have felt a bit more relaxed. As it was, the feeling of another dick in such close proximity, as well as the occasional, inevitable testicle bump as things progressed, was pretty damned unnerving as I lay, helplessly pinned down by Janine. If I'd had the option to quietly withdraw and slink away I might have taken it. If I hadn't liked and felt as comfortable with the couple in question I might also have done a runner. But I was, effectively, trapped and although I was way outside my comfort zone, I was, I have to confess, also slightly exhilarated by this unplanned breaking of new ground.

Once the initial awkwardness of getting into position was over and we were underway, my anxiety was replaced with powerful but conflicting emotions. I was so incredibly aware that some of the physical sensations I was feeling were those of another male member moving perilously close to mine. Alongside this were overwhelming waves of pleasure, both my own and those induced by the cataclysmic sights and sounds of Janine's. This was clearly a woman in her ultimate happy place and her euphoria was contagious. Deciding that I had nothing left to lose and everything to gain from getting as much out of this experience as I could, I let go of all remaining inhibition and embraced the moment, relaxing and just letting it happen around me while I tried to take it all in.

I lost count of the number of orgasms that Janine appeared to have; they seemed to blend into one another until it seemed like one endlessly flowing river of ecstasy. There was no way I could normally have held back for long with all that happening but perhaps the thought of coming right next to another guy was still clinging to the back of my mind because it seemed to be an age before the physical reflex overcame the mental barrier. When it finally happened, it was one of the most intense experiences I've ever had, coming in uncontrollable waves, perhaps all the more ferocious for having been held in denial for so long. Mercifully, Martin seemed to realise where I was at and by the time I had recovered enough to start to connect with reality once more, he had also finished and withdrawn and Janine collapsed onto my chest for a moment before rolling off to one side, thus relieving me of the need to contemplate my physical situation any further.

Both Janine and Martin were effusive in their gratitude for my participation and keen to know if I'd enjoyed it too. I had, and I told them so, but I suspect there must have been enough residual shock still lurking on my face to give them a clue that I was still processing it all. They offered more wine but, although I didn't wish to seem like I was rushing off or that I hadn't enjoyed our time, I declined. My head was buzzing and despite feeling fantastic I needed to get home where I could just chill out, contemplate this meet and assimilate how I felt about it in my own quiet space.

An hour later, settled comfortably on my sofa with a glass of my own wine, I ran back through the evening's events. Wow. The whole experience had hit me broadside and left me feeling a bit shell-shocked. I suppose some will think my reaction was overly squeamish but prior to all this I've always been a bit old school and, despite my more open and offbeat experiences over the last year, that's left me with some pretty ingrained perspectives. That's not to say I don't think it can

161

be a good thing to have your boundaries challenged every once in a while and as much as it had certainly confronted a few of my previous notions, I had to admit it had been one of the most sexually powerful experiences of my life. That said, whereas I would be open to doing the same again and perhaps be a little better prepared next time, I'd be pretty selective about who with and certainly it would have to be with an experienced couple. I don't think I'd have hesitated to pay Martin and Janine another visit and we did keep in touch for a while, but within a few months they'd transferred away with Martin's job and, although I would happily have travelled some distance to meet this couple, it just never quite happened. It remains one of my most intensely memorable encounters.

Couldn't Go For That

Whilst my head was still spinning from the events of the previous night, the very next day, 7th December, I had already arranged to meet Simon and Tracey for a drink at the Seven Stars pub near Petersfield and I was looking forward to meeting them. They didn't have any verifications but the photos on their profile looked pretty good and so long as they were truly representative, Tracey certainly appeared to be a head-turner in the looks department. We had exchanged mobile numbers and were flicking messages back and forth, with them suggesting that if the meet went well they'd be keen to come back to mine and hit the hot tub. It all seemed to be panning out nicely and I was getting some really good vibes. About an hour before we were due to meet, however, I got a text saying they were going to have to cancel as something unavoidable had come up. It was rather disappointing but these things happen so I took the opportunity to have a quiet evening and an early night.

I had a mildly apologetic text from them the next morning and we arranged to have another meet a couple of days later. Regrettably, exactly the same thing happened once again.

Once, fine. Twice, no. I accept that it might all have been legitimate but there's only so much time-wasting I can be bothered to put up with so I'm afraid I sent them a (mildly apologetic) message saying not to bother contacting me again.

David B

It was more than a little disappointing and quite a come-down from the giddy heights I'd been experiencing just a few days earlier.

Happy Holidays

Whilst I'd been messing about with Simon and Tracey, I'd also been in communication with Brian and Gail, a couple who live most of the year in Spain but had posted on their profile saying that they were on their way back to the UK for a few weeks and would be looking for meets while they were in the country. I got in touch the day they were due to arrive back and they replied almost immediately. We went on to exchange a couple of emails over the following day or two culminating in a decision to get together on the 9th of December. So far, my Yuletide efforts were keeping me pretty busy.

There were a couple of verifications on their profile but no pictures so my expectations really weren't very high but it was cold and bleak with not a great many better options available so a bit of friendly cavorting on an uninspiring December afternoon seemed appealing enough to be worth taking a chance on. I had plenty of wine at the ready in case it was needed to dampen down the senses, but it transpired that I needn't have worried about that. Brian and Gail seemed nice enough on first impressions, though it was Brian who did all the initial talking while Gail was a little quiet to start with. However, she far, far surpassed my expectations for general attractiveness, which was a pleasant and unexpected surprise. They'd listed themselves as in their fifties but, although I would have put Brian at the top end of that range, on appearances, I wouldn't have put Gail anywhere near it, more like mid-forties and very well-kept. I discovered that although they had been on the swinging scene for just over a year, because they lived abroad and only indulged when they were in the UK, they had only had a handful of encounters. As it was fairly damp and dark, I had lit a cheery fire and an assortment of candles. I'm not sure most guys would go to the trouble of bothering with candles but it was something Lynn used to love. I suppose I just got used to having them there when she was still around and in her absence I find their flickering presence pleasantly comforting. It's also quite a forgiving light which seems to generate a conducive atmosphere for getting people to be less self-conscious about taking off their clothes. I had to admit, despite my prior apprehension, I was now feeling quite enthusiastic about encouraging Gail out of hers.

As it turned out, they were naturists, one reason they had opted to move abroad, so getting them out of their clothes proved to be no problem at all. After a fairly brief chat and barely a start on the wine, Brian made the welcome suggestion that Gail should loosen her top so that we could both admire her cleavage whilst we all chatted. I was at that happy stage where I felt completely relaxed with the situation, excited about the impending scenario and utterly comfortable with the company. The conversation started hinting flirtatiously at the fun that was to come and Gail, seemingly having lost her earlier reticence soon had us all removing bits of clothing in the glowing fireside sanctuary that was my sitting room. We were all lounging quite casually on my sofa, Gail reclining between me and Brian. As the flirting continued, some gentle touching and stroking began, leading to some good natured snogging between me and Gail and the gradual removal of the rest of the clothing, giving me an opportunity to explore the enticingly peachy breasts which had been partially on display for some time now. We decided to move things upstairs to the bedroom and Brian asked if I was ok with him filming. I was getting quite used to that question cropping up. It seems to be something a lot of people want to do. In any case, it doesn't bother me so I was quite happy to oblige him. It's funny when people are filming, usually it makes me feel, if anything, less self-conscious than someone just looking on would, perhaps because it forms a kind of barrier, but in this case it proved to be a bit tricky. Possibly, Brian was something of an enthusiast. Either that or he fancied himself as a potential porn film-maker. In any case, he appeared to be trying to get every possible angle covered, although it wasn't giving me the impression of being particularly artistic in its perspective.

Having made a good start on Gail's upper anatomy in the sitting room, once upstairs, I'd started exploring her with my fingers, marvelling at how wet she'd become with just the minimal warm up we'd had. She returned the favour and we had a few minutes of mutually encouraging play before I manoeuvred myself on top of her and took the plunge. For the most part, I was fairly switched off to the camera, happily focusing on Gail's welcoming form, but after a while Brian's antics became positively intrusive. It seemed everywhere I looked, he was there with his little camera on full zoom, sometimes getting so up close and personal I feared he might actually lose the camera altogether. I admit, I raised an eyebrow once or twice but since he was happily allowing me to indulge myself with his wife I felt inclined to keep my mouth shut. That became rather more difficult, though, when he started interjecting his own words of encouragement in the style of a would-be movie producer, all the while tracking in and out with his wretched camera. I could see a shadow of displeasure forming in Gail's eyes which built rapidly and before long she'd told him in no uncertain terms to shut the hell up and give it a rest with the camera. In fairness to him, he did back off and put the camera aside although the directional interjections still persisted.

Feeling a new sense of freedom, having been liberated from performing for the camera, I started ploughing hard into Gail, feeling her respond enthusiastically, moaning and writhing around, volume rising, her nails clawing into my back as

167

she eventually climaxed. What happened next really did startle me though.

I'd taken a late decision to withdraw, once Gail was done, with the intention of finishing myself off over her. She was quick to bring me up to her mouth, helping me along with her tongue before pulling away and compressing her breasts together, indicating her desire for me to decorate them, which I did with pleasure. She then began playing with the overspill, massaging it over her breasts then taking the residues down below, working it around her clit. This sight obviously stimulated Brian in some way because the next thing I knew, he was going down on Gail, getting a good mouthful of my jungle juice in the process. She seemed just fine with that, in fact she seemed, perhaps, to expect it so maybe it was just his thing and she knew that. Hard to tell and I certainly wasn't going to ask. It's just not something that would appeal to me to do under any circumstances and I found it bizarre to watch although I try not to question another person's preferences, especially when I have just had sex with their wife! In any case, bizarre interludes aside, it seemed to have been a satisfactory session all round and we agreed, since it was still quite early, to pop out to the hot tub for a chill out and a chat. Brian helped himself to another bottle of wine on his way through the kitchen which slightly irked me as it would have been nice to be asked, though I would have offered anyway. After half an hour or so of chatting, I came to the conclusion that Brian was actually a fairly arrogant sort of person, not someone whose company I would probably choose ordinarily. Gail, on the other hand, was absolutely lovely; sweet, funny and extremely pleasant to talk to. I felt quite a connection with her which was probably why, somewhat against my better judgement, I agreed to meet with them again.

Sexually speaking, round two was a better experience than the first meet. They came to my house again and Brian, far from his previous movie-maker persona, appeared to have lost all interest, rapidly retiring to the garden where he huddled against the cold with a fag and a bottle of wine. Having learned my lesson on our previous encounter, I had taken the precaution of hiding the nicer bottles away, leaving the less expensive selection for Brian's perusal. He occasionally glanced in to watch idly through the garden doors but seemed distant and uninterested. I could tell he was not so happy with the situation this time but, frankly, that didn't bother me too much as I hadn't taken to him at all and rather resented his overbearing nature, particularly towards Gail, whom I just felt quite sorry for in being stuck with him. It made me determined to give her as good a time as possible. For variety, we'd based ourselves in the kitchen this time, which at least gave Brian a reason to stay in the garden, which was infinitely preferable to having him follow us upstairs and potentially get his camera out again. Inspired by previous encounters, I'd invested in one or two playful items which I decided I would bring down to see if Gail was interested. She seemed slightly amused but happy to go along with me on it so I left them in easy reach and decided to see how things worked out. I loved her lack of inhibition about getting naked but I'd managed to persuade her to keep her clothes on long enough to allow me the opportunity to take them off her myself, which I did slowly and carefully, one item at a time, relishing the enticing, piece-by-piece exposure. Having revealed her completely, I laid her gently back across the island butcher's block in the middle of the kitchen and, with her permission, loosely handcuffed her to handles on either side. She seemed absolutely fine with that so I asked her if she would be ok if I blindfolded her too. She giggled a bit but let me do it anyway. I guess she must have trusted me as I'm not sure I would necessarily agree to be handcuffed to a butcher's block in a near stranger's kitchen, just in case they suddenly turned out to be a raging psychopath, although, I suspect, despite his detachment, that Brian would have come to her rescue if that had proved to be the case in this instance...

Blindfold applied, I began to stroke and caress her; arms, legs, belly, neck then breasts and nipples. She started out a little bit giggly and twitchy but after a while seemed to settle into it and by the time I began on her breasts I could tell she was relaxed, no twitching, just an arching of her back and barely audible sigh as I took her nipples into my mouth. I spent some time enjoying those before sliding my hand down over her belly where, no surprise this time, I found her incredibly wet and responsive. Keeping my hands moving over her body, I shifted down to the end of the block and stood between her legs, firmly but gently pushing them further apart, rubbing my length against her a few times, coating myself with her juices before changing angle and sliding inside her. She gasped and arched back, I can only assume it was with pleasure since we were so well lubricated she can barely have felt me enter. The block is a good height for these activities but the base does get in the way of your knees and mine were killing me from the bumping and bashing after only about five minutes so, much as it almost seemed a shame to stop the beginner's S&M party, I un-cuffed her, leaving the blindfold on, and took her over to the stairs where I placed her hands on the fifth step up and moved in from behind. It was an immense improvement in the comfort department and the added benefit of leaving the blindfold on was that she hadn't seen Brian's slightly disapproving look coming at us from the other side of the doors. She was very game and didn't seem to mind the stairs at all. I contemplated taking her upstairs for a little bedroom time but I had a strong suspicion that Brian would have been up there after us like a rocket and, frankly, I preferred him at his current distance. By the time I'd seen that thought process through, Gail was showing signs of climaxing anyway so I continued where we were and, with a little manual help on her clit she came soon afterwards. Remembering how our previous encounter had ended, I focused on getting myself to release inside her as quickly as possible, finding the thought of a Parka-clad Brian rushing in from the cold to lick my man juice off Gail an extremely unappealing idea. I felt quite an affection for Gail, partly because she seemed such a genuinely nice person but also because she had to put up with Buccaneer Brian all the time and for that she had my deepest sympathy. My assessment of him had not softened one iota on second meeting and in my opinion she deserved sainthood for sticking with him.

To my surprise, given Brian's general demeanour on that second encounter, we went on to meet one further time before Christmas. This time I headed over to their modest but pleasant Surrey house on a Thursday afternoon. I could immediately tell that Brian had been on the vino before I arrived. Aside from answering the door stark naked, he was overtly jovial and plainly quite drunk although he soon pottered off, apparently quite happily, to do his own thing, which I believe involved sitting in their study at his computer although I have no idea what he was actually doing. Editing his home movies perhaps? And so it was that I got to spend another hour or two, to all intents and purposes alone, with the lovely Gail. She had obviously decided it was her turn to take charge this time, steering me into their sitting room where she undressed me, and herself, of course, but I just let her get on with it this time. Quite honestly, I was amazed that she'd kept any clothes on at all when Brian had already disrobed. Having bypassed the need for preamble by this stage, she got stuck in straight away and treated me to a mind-bendingly good blow job. It was an untypically sunny day and the rare shafts of light falling across me as I reclined on the sofa were surprisingly warm. It was really quite blissful. Yielding to my desire to embrace the moment and trusting my appendage's almost unfailing determination to give me more than a single shot at the target, I let her take me all the way to the brink and over the edge, just for the sheer pleasure of releasing to her in such an unexpectedly perfect setting. I got the sense she was a bit surprised that I'd gone to that point so soon but she allowed me to switch places with her so that I could let my tongue loose on her in my turn. I nearly always find that this will rekindle my state of readiness and, fortunately, today everything ran true to form and within a fairly short space of time he was raring to go once more. As this capacity for resurrection hadn't been something Gail had been previously aware of, she was slightly surprised but, I think, very pleased and we had a rather lovely romp, without intrusion, as the late afternoon sun went down.

I was a little sad to say goodbye when it was over as I knew that they were unlikely to have any further opportunities to meet up again before heading back to Spain shortly after Christmas but I was grateful for Gail's generous contribution to my seasonal festivities. I've had no further contact with them but I do find a smile sliding onto my face whenever I think about those sessions with Gorgeous Gail.

It also made me feel very glad that although my marriage had been cut so savagely short, at least it had been happy and cohesive while it lasted and I suddenly had a powerful sense that my short but intensely happy marital experience was infinitely preferable to a longer but less perfect one.

Serena Sex Bomb

The Seven Stars pub, just outside Petersfield, is a venue I've used several times for first meets. It's easy to find and very nice inside with lots of nooks and crannies to position yourself in, giving a better chance of having a chat without feeling conspicuous or being overheard. Particularly useful sometimes if the conversation gets down to the nitty-gritty quite quickly which occasionally it does. I had suggested it for a meet between myself and a newly-contacted couple, Maurice and Serena. I didn't know a great deal about them and there were only body shots of Serena, nothing of Maurice at all, but they had some good verifications on their profile and I suspected it might be the classic situation of older, unfit man married to younger, well-kept woman and things had got a bit stale in the bedroom. As it turned out, I was spot on with the exception that, in fact, he actually had great difficulty getting ready for action, as it were, and she had become just a little bit frustrated.

I arrived at the appointed time of nine o'clock, grabbed a drink and found a suitably private place to sit, although this was achieved with some difficulty as it was extremely busy there that night. I was glad to have found a table at all but especially so when it turned out to be one of those meets that gets verbally down to business pretty much straight away. No sooner had I sat down than Maurice appeared, introduced himself and explained that he and Serena had been dining in the restaurant but would be over very shortly. I had about ten minutes to settle in and enjoy my drink before they returned, bearing a fresh round of drinks, to join me.

My first thought on seeing Serena was genuinely 'Wow'! She was tall, dark haired and the plunging cleavage revealed by her top hinted at a gorgeously curvy body lurking under her tailored jacket and skirt. She looked fabulous and she moved in the strong, seductive way of a very fit and confident woman. Maurice was, by contrast short, round and a little baggy, a similar age to Serena but I would surmise that he had let himself go a bit. It is incredible how often I have come across this scenario on the swinging scene and it amazes me that so many guys with gorgeous wives have let things get to this stage. Perhaps they don't realise how lucky they are to have a woman who looks after herself and keeps herself fit. How lucky they are to have a wife at all, in fact, let alone one who is still firing on all cylinders and looking damn good into the bargain. It mystifies me.

Serena was lively, funny and engaging, making easy conversation with a decidedly flirty edge from the start, smiling and making full, intense eye contact. Maurice sort of blobbed about on the periphery, amiable but not really contributing much to the general flow, although, later on, he would occasionally interject some comment or other when the conversation began to touch on our potential for future encounters. By this time, Serena had my full attention, not least due to her habit of crossing and uncrossing her lusciously long legs at regular intervals, her skirt riding higher each time, her teasing smile making it perfectly obvious she knew exactly what she was doing. I am a sucker for a woman who has the confidence to tease like that, it promises so many wonderful things and I was almost instantly smitten. I did try to bring Maurice into the fold. Really, I did make quite an effort, mostly because I was by now very much hoping he was going to willingly let me fuck his wife. You've got to like at least that much about a man who is prepared to even consider letting such a thing happen. But my efforts with him were largely in vain.

Hints at what they were looking for were coming through almost from the start. There were quite a few people standing near our table when we had first introduced ourselves but they began to thin out and we were soon able to bring things up more openly. Within an hour of arriving at the pub, our conversation had covered pretty much everything we needed to discuss about what we all were looking for from a meet. On the whole this momentum was fuelled by Serena, who seemed encouragingly self-assured about what she wanted and more than happy to discuss it in detail. I lapped up the information, ever more eager and hopeful that I was going to get to play with this one. Essentially, she simply wanted to be comprehensively satisfied in the standard ways in the absence of her husband's ability to do so. This was, of course, all discussed in front of the watchful Maurice, who was very difficult to read but if I'd had to call it there and then I would have said that he hadn't particularly taken to me, although he wasn't giving me any real sense of animosity. I was inclined to stay and enjoy Serena's company at some length but, as the evening progressed I started to feel a shift in Maurice's attitude and openness. He became gruffer and rather withdrawn, giving little to indicate that he was up for this at all. Trying to shelve my disappointment at the thought that I might not be gifted permission to satisfy Serena's current sexual deficit and not particularly hopeful of any further progression on that basis, I decided to cut my losses and head home. Serena looked a little surprised when I announced that I was off, but gave me a smile and an affectionate hug. Maurice growled a bit, which I vaguely interpreted as a goodbye, seeming barely able to raise his eyes to meet mine.

I pondered their situation on my journey back, wondering again at any man's lack of motivation to get his butt in shape with a wife like that and feeling rather deprived knowing that I was unlikely to get to play with the adorable Serena. To my surprise and utter delight by the time I got home I'd had a voicemail and was thrilled to hear Serena's voice on the message saying that they would love to meet again and, this time, play. That brought a very large smile to my face, an uplifting end to what had been a fairly enjoyable evening in its own right.

As they were both commuting daily to London and they obviously had a pretty good social life too, I knew that finding time for a meet might prove a little tricky so I was pleased when they suggested a playdate within a week, namely a one hour slot at mine at seven o'clock on the following Saturday evening. I suppose that might sound a bit demanding, clinical even, to someone reading this. It suited me fine though, a 'drop in, fuck and go', nice and early which would leave me with time to meet up with friends later. It was ideal.

They arrived at my house at five to seven the following Saturday. I'd had a slight sense of trepidation about how Maurice was going to be after his stilted interaction at our evening in the pub but I was so tantalised by the thought of playing with Serena that I can't say I let it bother me great deal. She looked so fabulous standing on my doorstep in her tight little black dress that I almost forgot Maurice was even there until he stepped out from behind her and came forward to shake hands. He was perfectly civil, if not exactly friendly. Knowing they were on a tight time limit we headed straight upstairs where Serena had unzipped and stepped out of her dress in an instant. The sight of her in her skimpy black thong and low cut bra, all womanly curves, heavenly breasts and perfect skin, was a sight to behold and confess I stood there for a second, gawping in admiration, briefly stunned into inaction by the sudden appearance of this perfect, gorgeous woman in my bedroom. She smiled, evidently pleased at my reaction and said in a husky seductive voice 'come on then, show me what you've got and let's see if you know what to do with it'. 'Yes, come on Dave, let's get things moving', added Maurice, with a 'time is money' kind of tone in his voice. It wasn't much of an enhancement to the atmosphere but there was nothing I could do about that now so I just did my best to block out his presence. I'd been on a hot edge all day anticipating this moment. Somehow, the slight pressure of knowing it would be a brief session added to the tension and the poor fella had pretty much had a semi on since breakfast.

The sight of Serena's half naked body brought on a very rapid response and I was immediately rearing up and begging for the relief of being liberated. Serena came straight forward and, unbuttoning me, released the pressure that had been painfully building up before dropping to her knees and with her eyes on mine and a smile still on her lips taking me in her mouth, working on me sensuously and with focused dedication. I was already quite tightly wound and the sight of her head bobbing away down there, dark, wavy hair swinging in unison, had me fighting to retain control almost immediately. After a few minutes, needing a breather before she made my brain implode, I eased her up onto the bed, sliding aside the barely-there thong before going down. That gave me a moment to reign in my runaway enthusiasm as well as to appreciate the perfection of what I was about to enjoy. She was utterly flawless, her skin rapturously smooth. The feel of it under my hands as I stroked her legs and up her silky thighs was as energising as the taste and feel of her on my tongue. My thoughts eventually, inevitably, turned to her breasts and I had to investigate, discovering that her skin and shape was as perfect above as it was below, pierced nipples a surprising addition to the arrangement and intriguing to explore as they seemed to make her shiver whenever I sucked on them or my tongue lightly flicked and played with them.

Maurice was sitting in my bedroom armchair, trousers down but not off, watching but seeming distant, limp dick in his hand. I couldn't help but feel a bit sad for him, as I always do with this kind of scenario, and I felt a mild pang of understanding towards his rather unfriendly gruffness. It can't be the easiest of situations to handle but all power to him for not letting his incapacity stop his wife having some fun. I'm certain Serena was grateful for that and I certainly was too.

Sliding my hand between her sheeny, satin thighs, I found her invitingly wet. She moaned and tensed as I slid inside her and began to rock back and forth, slowly at first but building pace with her responses until I was pummelling her hard, leaning down to suck on those nipple piercings from time to time which had her thrashing around like a wild animal. I could have fucked her for hours but it wasn't long before she came, quite violently. Not wanting to miss the boat, knowing we didn't have much time, I let that tip me over too. It was a short but intense, extremely satisfying session. Perhaps not surprisingly it didn't appear to me that Maurice felt the same. Doubtless he would have preferred to be doing the job himself, my services having only been drafted in as emergency cover. I do sometimes wonder why someone in his situation wouldn't use Viagra, but I know there are health issues for some people with that and I suspect, from my experience with couples, that in many cases the inclusion of a third party is something desired by the active partner regardless. Unfortunately, Maurice's slightly glowering expression cast a slight pall over things and I started to feel pretty uncomfortable. I was glad we were in my house, not theirs. Within a short while we'd said our goodbyes and they had headed off for their dinner party, leaving me to enjoy my satisfied relief in peace. I closed the door behind them, put on some music and spent a few minutes tidying up before heading down to the pub for a well-earned pint and a catch-up with my neighbours. On the walk there, reflecting on the evening's activities, I decided, on balance, that, much as I'd adored Serena and relished every bit of our brief encounter, I really didn't think I could relax with the oppressive presence of Maurice lurking in the corner. There are some people who seem to have the capacity to affect everyone in their vicinity with their mood. Maurice was definitely one of those and I not only pitied Serena for having to deal with it but was reluctant to expose myself to any more of it from him.

I really wasn't expecting that he would feel much like exposing himself to any more of my cavorting with his wife either but, to my surprise, I got a message from them within a few days asking if I'd like to meet again. I struggled a little, the memory of Serena's silky breasts and thighs still so fresh in my mind, but, perhaps unusually, reason prevailed. It was a tough call, I'd have loved another play with Serena, but I was having a very busy time with other meets so I guess I felt the sacrifice was bearable on that basis.

David B

Lolita

My next encounter was a bit of a Christmas bonus. Although it didn't occur as the result of a specific interaction on a particular website, it did happen as a result of the other party's awareness that I was engaging in this new lifestyle and her interest in finding out more about it.

It was now the 16th of December and I was heading out to a birthday gathering at a pub not far from where I live. The birthday girl was someone I knew reasonably well but who was not in my immediate group of friends so I wasn't sure I'd know many other people there. As it happened, there were a few people I recognised and, by all accounts, a few who recognised me too. Everyone seemed in a very festive mood, and it was one of those nights where I ended up staying for longer than I'd intended or expected to. I'm extremely glad I did. Not only was it a great night in good company, but when the party started winding down I was approached by a woman I hadn't met before but who had, evidently, been talking to someone she had met there that night who had let her in on my little secret.

She introduced herself to me as Helen, and explained that she, along with her friend, Marcie, were very keen to talk to me, as the swinging scene was something they'd been considering getting involved with for quite some time but were a bit apprehensive about. At first I thought they meant that they were together and wanting to get involved on that basis, which led to some initial embarrassment on my part, but, having established that they meant to do this separately as

single women looking for male partners, I felt better
equipped to offer them a little insight and guidance.

I suppose Helen would have been in her late twenties, perhaps twenty eight or nine, an attractive, bubbly blonde. Marcie was rather younger, around twenty two or three, dark
haired and with impishly mischievous eyes. Both of them
were sparky and funny and since we'd all had a fair bit to
drink by this time we ended up having an hilariously entertaining and candid chat, covering the basics of how my brand
of swinging works, which sites were the best to use, how to
avoid dodgy profiles, etc. I did tell them about one or two of
my encounters to illustrate my points and they were obviously finding the whole idea very appealing. They were hungry
for information and clearly genuinely interested in getting
started. Helen booked a taxi which turned up while we were
still mid flow and on the spur of an alcohol fuelled moment I
invited them back to my house, offering to show them
around a couple of the websites I use if they were interested.
They were both up for that so we all jumped into the cab and
headed back to the cottage. Not expecting to have been out
for so long, I'd left the fire burning with a guard in front.
Fortunately, it still hadn't quite gone out and I was quickly
able to resurrect its warming glow to keep us company, along
with a nice bottle of wine, while we perused various sites and
profiles. The girls had many questions and wanted to hear
more stories. I explained about the hot tub and how it had
contributed to my experience, regaling them with the story of
my neighbour's abortive attempt to spy on us. They fell
about laughing and, rather carried away by the atmosphere
and wine, I asked if they'd like to sample the hot tub while
they were here. Bearing in mind it was December, they were
surprisingly keen to take me up on that offer. Perhaps the
subject matter of our conversations had titillated them a little. Anyhow, without hesitation, they embraced the idea so I
went out to take the cover off the tub, leaving them to strip

off and hop in while I collected the wine and glasses before joining them.

It was the second time in the tub for me that day, as I'd had a little bob in there when I got home from work, adding, at the time, a good handful of lavender crystals to help soothe my aching shoulders. Perhaps Helen was susceptible to the remains of those because within fifteen minutes she was starting to nod off and took herself inside, wrapped in a huge towel, later to be found fast asleep on the sofa in front of the fire. Marcie, however, did not appear to be feeling any such effect, still bright as a button and eager to hear another tale or two. Whether or not it was the effect of hearing the stories, the prospect of getting into swinging, the wine or the ever-conducive effect of the hot tub bubbles, I couldn't say, but something had obviously got her in the mood for a bit of naughtiness. There was the usual touch of skin and limbs under the water but then it's not a huge tub so I didn't think too much of it. Gradually, though, I started to feel that there was rather more bumping than the occasional, casual graze, and my radar came instantly to life. I was suddenly aware of the distinct touch of a hand on my thigh and just as the realisation that the radar reading was correct fully registered, she suddenly turned and positively launched herself towards me through the water.

Without wishing to sound inept, I was slightly taken aback for a second, purely because I was aware that this lovely lass was considerably younger than me and in all honesty, I actually hadn't anticipated this turn of events at all. My mind briefly tried to process a couple of 'right or wrong's and 'should or shouldn'ts' but, quite frankly, with a naked, frisky twenty two year old slithering her little wet body against mine and kissing me with such refreshingly nubile urgency, I was toast. The best I could do was try to accommodate her evident desire, which I was, obviously, happy to do, without imposing anything on her. I didn't dare take a lead or call a shot, somehow feeling a bit vulnerable in this unexpected situation. After the initial surprise, Percy the Water Dragon was quick to react to this latest turn of events, rapidly raising his head to prod my assailant firmly in the belly. Grinning, arms wrapped round my neck, she lifted herself up then eased herself down, little by little, until she had taken the sublimely delighted Percy completely in and was rocking him gently in the deep. A part of my head was saying 'yikes, Dave, should you be doing this?' but the rest of it, by far the majority, was having a party worthy of the Rio carnival. What a fabulous turn of events to warm a cold winter's night.

Marcie was crooning away and seemed perfectly happy so I just let her get on and do her thing while I allowed myself to relax a bit and just enjoy all the different sensations this was giving me, physical and mental. She seemed to be quite content where she was, in control and away in her own little world. She gradually worked up a bit of pace, opening her eyes as it built and pulling herself towards me, exquisite breasts with their delicate nipples bouncing in front of my eyes until I managed to catch one and close my lips around it. She threw back her head and her rhythm slowed and deepened as she appeared to be approaching her climax. I half watched her, keen to know where she was at, but the other half of my brain was far away in a distant happy place, surrendered to this unplanned but glorious experience. Her face gave away the critical moment but I could have guessed anyway, her already tight space constricting even further as she contracted over and over, requiring virtually no movement to bring me off too.

We stayed there for a few minutes, rocking gently back and forth, her head resting on my shoulder, then suddenly I felt her shoulders start to shake and was momentarily concerned that she was crying. Gently pushing her back far enough to see her face, I found, to my abject relief that she was, in fact, giggling, apparently at her own naughtiness, which continued

183

as she began to disengage herself. I quickly jumped out of the tub and grabbed towels, catching and wrapping her in one the moment she left the water as it was late now and really cold, frost visibly settling on the surfaces around us. I hustled her inside and rubbed her down, which made her giggle even more. Leaving her to get dressed, I pulled my towel tight around me and raced back out into the chilly night to cover the tub before hurrying back inside and up- stairs to finish drying myself off and find a warm bathrobe. By the time I came back down, it was to find both girls fast asleep, one on the sofa, one in the armchair. Perhaps not too surprisingly as it was by now nearly three in the morning. Helen looked pretty comfortable on the sofa but I wasn't convinced that Marcie was in a good place for a proper sleep. I shook her gently and, when she stirred, firmly propelled her upstairs to the spare room and settled her into bed. I left a glass of water on the table beside Helen and a note letting her that know that Marcie was upstairs in the spare room, popped a blanket over her and left her to sleep. Taking water up for the already comatose Marcie too, I finally fell into bed and slipped into a contented sleep myself.

As the events of the previous night sifted gradually into my waking consciousness the next morning, I couldn't help smil- ing to myself. What a situation to wind up in. Thinking I'd better check on the girls, I got up, heading first to the spare room to see if Marcie was alright. She wasn't there but I could hear the sound of whispering and hushed giggles drift- ing up the stairs from the sitting room. I headed down to find them huddled in duvets on the sofa, seemingly in good spirits, so left them while I went off to make us all coffee. Marcie obviously had no qualms whatsoever about divulging her antics in the tub to Helen and there was a lot of good natured banter pinging back and forth. Much to my relief, all was well. I decided that I must have been a very, very good boy in some way that year for Santa to have come along and given me such an amazing surprise gift.

We exchanged numbers before they headed off home after finishing their coffee and that was that. I have heard from both of them since then, as they each created profiles and sent me messages via the website to let me know. I'm not aware if they've ventured out on any meets and, in the circumstances, I felt it would be better to let them suggest meeting me again if either of them wanted to. I really hope they are having as good an experience with it as I have if they've decided to pursue it.

Life is full of surprises and my impromptu get together with these two girls was one of the better and more enjoyable ones.

David B

Old Smokey

For my next venture, I met up with Trevor and Lisa in the bar at the Marriott hotel just outside Portsmouth on the 17th of December and, so far as first meets go, it seemed okay. There was a niggling doubt in the back of my mind about something but I couldn't quite put my finger on it so I just went along with their suggestion to meet up and we agreed to get together for a playdate a couple of days later, the plan being for them to come over to mine for the evening. They asked if they could stay over but I declined, making an excuse about having to leave early the next morning. Maybe it was intuition but, for whatever reason, I just didn't feel comfortable with the idea. I made my usual efforts for a winter meet, lighting candles and the log fire as well as selecting what I hoped was conducive music and opening some wine which I began to sip at while I waited for them to arrive.

I was a bit disgruntled when they turned up on my doorstep both smoking roll-ups. It's all a matter of personal taste and each to their own but I don't happen to like the smell or taste of cigarette smoke and I thought I'd made it pretty clear on my profile that I am very much in the non-smoking/non-smokers category. I wonder why some people just ignore stuff like that. If you smoke, that's fine, but say so; don't try to lie or deceive, it's just not going to help achieve a happy outcome. Perhaps they assumed that most people will be too polite to just tell them to go away or shut the door in their face. Certainly, I find it difficult to be that pragmatic so I did let them in but it wasn't the best start and I was incredibly glad they weren't going to be staying over. We sat and talked for a while and they quickly started laying down ground rules for our play time, which is fine, of course, but it was something that could easily have been talked through at our first meet where, in fact, they'd had ample opportunity. Even if the location of the first meet turns out not to be suitable for an open chat, if there are rules or criteria that need to be discussed or agreed it would seem natural to broach the subject in messages before the actual meet.

I suppose it was the fact that we had got this far, plus not wanting to completely waste an evening, that made me try not to let my reactions show and to agree to their requests. After a little more preamble, Trevor suggested it was time for me to get busy with Lisa and, as I wasn't enjoying their verbal company to any great degree, it seemed like a good plan to me. I asked them for their preference of location and it was no big surprise when they opted for the bedroom so up we went.

One of the rules they'd issued was that I was not to kiss Lisa, which was absolutely fine in the circumstances as the smoking left me with no great desire to do so anyway. They'd also stipulated no nipple touching, hair touching, general stroking or finger penetration. It seemed bizarrely restrictive and not the easiest list to stick to. In a growing state of disbelief at how this meet was progressing, I decided I'd just humour them and see how things worked out. Obviously, they weren't a particularly adventurous couple, at least not with a third party. Lisa stood with her back to us while she undressed, her disappointingly sensible underwear still firmly in place when she eventually turned around, the rest of her clothes piled on the chair. Her body language had implied that she preferred to do this herself so I left her to it while I removed my own outer clothes, mirroring her level of nakedness by keeping my boxer shorts on and my socks too, since I wasn't wearing a bra. It was a minor and slightly silly nod, on my part, to the rather irritating quirkiness of this meet. There was then a palpable sense of awkwardness as we stood there, all seemingly waiting for someone to make the first move. Or, perhaps, they were just waiting for me to take my socks off, it was hard to tell. Somehow the ice needed to be broken but the list of restrictions left me with relatively few options for an opening gambit. I wasn't even certain if she intended to keep her underwear on for the entire duration and whether I might get a slap, from her, or possibly from Trevor, if I tried to remove it. Something, however, had to give so I braced myself, took a few steps towards her and took her hand (surely that was allowed?), leading her towards the bed where, thankfully, she positioned herself without me having to touch anything.

Not sure how to proceed from here, I hesitated, wondering how I was going to warm this chilly girl up, or myself for that matter, with so few tools at my disposal. I was about to stop trying to second guess the situation and simply ask outright if it was alright to help her out of her underwear when Trevor sprang (relatively speaking) into action, got onto the bed beside Lisa and began some sort of foreplay with her which, happily, involved the removal of her uninspiringly plain knickers and bra. Unfortunately, it also involved a few of Trevor's coverings coming off too, which was fine, of course, but I hoped this wasn't going to turn into a voyeur-only session since the thought of watching Trevor getting down and dirty with Lisa on my bed left me cold. Unsure how things were going to turn out, I skulked in the corner nearest the door, declining to watch too closely while Trevor stoked the flames of Lisa's presumably present but well-hidden furnace.

Unfortunately, I wasn't finding this situation very arousing and was in no way yet ready for any action that might eventually come my way. I had started debating whether to take matters into my own hands, as it were, so as to be prepared, just in case, or whether to just leave and let them get on with it, when Trevor rolled himself over and announced his opinion that Lisa was now ready for a bit of interaction with me.

I was caught off guard, but the thought of getting Trevor off my bed and getting a bit of action myself into the bargain galvanised me and I decided to give it my best shot. I turned my attention to the now naked form of Lisa and was surprised to find that Trevor had apparently done quite a good job. She lay back on the pillows, arms loosely up beside her head and legs spread revealing a plainly well prepared and lubricated entry point. It might not sound too alluring but, given my ever-decreasing expectations over the past hour, it was something of a pleasure to behold. To my relief, I felt a corresponding tell-tale twitch of appreciation from the beast below and, giving him no chance to argue, approached Lisa, clumsily positioning myself over her while trying, in essence, not to touch her at all, anywhere, in order not to break any of the rules. To my increasing surprise she seemed really receptive, arching herself up against me then pulling her knees up and wrapping her legs loosely around my back, eyes closed but clearly good to go. Tentatively, I started to move against her, hoping to induce the requisite level of engagement required on my part to get to the next stage. Mission accomplished reasonably quickly, I began to edge inside her, gently to begin with, but almost immediately with increasing pace and depth in response to her own vigorous movements, her huffs and gasps telling me that she, at least, was enjoying the experience. While I was barely into my stride, without warning, she came, though it would have been easy to miss. Two squeaks and it was over. Surprised, but hopeful that there was more to come, I kept moving gently until Trevor basically told me to hop off as she'd need a break. And he was right, she did need a break. A cigarette break!

She and Trevor skipped off to the garden and came back a few minutes later stinking of smoke but ready to get going again. I was bemused and not in the best humour by now but things were still pretty perky down below and I thought I might get a better crack at it second time in. I was wrong. A short warm up to get us back in the groove and hey presto, within moments she'd come again and was off, hot footing it down the stairs for another fag leaving me open-mouthed and incredulous.

Third time lucky? Apparently not. Away she went again and this time I'd had enough. Three-nil was a harsh enough score when there was no sign of a potential goal for me or even a unbiased referee to see fair play. I had lost all patience with the whole game and, as politely as possible, sent them packing.

I don't suppose, if there is a standard at all, that my attitude to swinging is necessarily representative of the norm but, to me, swinging, as with sex in general, is a shared experience, a matter of give and take, not about an individual getting their satisfaction at the expense of another. I know what is on offer with this lifestyle and I know that it in no way represents a relationship in the classic sense, but it still doesn't work unless both, or all, sets of needs are being met and, as with relationships of any kind, disrespect is a sure-fire way to make it all go pear-shaped pretty damn fast.

Amazingly, despite telling them why I wasn't happy on the night and making it clear this particular scenario wasn't going to work for me, they texted and messaged me numerous times afterwards asking for another meet. Some people just want to play by their own rules and struggle to take no for an answer, but a 'no' it very firmly and emphatically was from me.

Santa's Coming!

Following a flurry of promising emails, I'd arranged to meet up with Juliet for the next instalment of my 'Merry Christmas, Dave' project, at the Old Thorns Golf and Country Club in the small Hampshire village of Liphook. It's a very nice venue, although, as with most places, likely to be very busy as it was now less than a week before Christmas. Perhaps it was that thought which prompted Juliet's request that we have coffee at my house instead of the planned public meet.

She arrived mid-afternoon but shunned the coffee, requesting a glass of wine instead. We chatted for well over an hour before she said she had to go. As she was getting ready to leave, she came up and gave me a good old-fashioned kiss along with an unexpected and surprisingly firm squeeze of the old trouser tackle before saying that she'd very much like to come back for play time as soon as possible. Once I'd peeled my eyebrows off the ceiling and composed myself, I suggested a few dates, one of which happened to be Boxing Day. It turned out she was free and more than happy to fill the time with some fun. Good news! That gave me something to look forward to, a little incentive to get me through the still-daunting prospect of Christmas.

Christmas Day arrived and, eventually, passed. With the appropriate family festivities safely negotiated, and, to some degree enjoyed, I spent the afternoon of Boxing Day preparing and looking forward to the rather less standard-issue festivities planned for that evening. Juliet arrived at about six thirty, the misty drizzle lighting up like a halo over her head in the porch light. My own little Christmas angel! I rushed her straight through to the sitting room to warm herself by the fire, leaving her there for a moment while I went to get her a drink. She had just started to unbutton her coat when I returned so I reached to help her off with it, rewarded for my efforts by the sight of her emerging in a miniscule, fur-trimmed Santa dress which I can only say was probably not one that many women would dare to wear out in public. Indecently short, with bare skin showing at the sides and white fluff across the top, which barely concealed anything. It caught me completely by surprise but what an incredibly welcome one. After a five-year series of stilted, half-hearted Christmases, I needed an alternative to buck the trend and lift me out of the mire. Juliet certainly looked promisingly like she might fulfil that need and this Christmas had taken an instant turn for the better. Ho ho ho!

We sat on the sofa for a while, sipping our drinks in an incongruously civilised manner, given the circumstances, but I couldn't keep the smile off my face or my eyes off the top of her dress. Surely that fluff was tickling her barely concealed nipples? Mentally, it was tickling me too. Unable to keep my hands off it any longer, I reached over to stroke my finger through the white tendrils, revealing, as I had suspected, the tiniest hint of an areola peeping out from below. Drawing the back of my finger along the line again, it took no pressure to lower it further, exposing a delectable nipple in the process. Drink in hand, sitting quite still, she grinned and dropped her eyes to where my naughty finger was quietly stroking, tracing outlines, pushing further, switching to the other side, until both her breasts were fully visible in all their fur-framed glory. Pausing briefly to relieve her of her wine glass, I set mine down too leaving hands and mouth then free to explore fully. Settling herself back on the sofa, she let me play, unhindered, her breathing and occasional sighs suggesting she was quite content. Before long, my hands were making their way further down over the velvety fabric, fingers slipping under the edge where it gave way to the exposed skin at her waist, savouring the silky sensation as I reached further through to capture the curve of a buttock.

Shifting just a little, she brought my face up to hers and kissed me, full and long, then reached down to unzip me, much to my relief as things had been getting uncomfortably tight down there. The Rudolf-themed boxers which were my token contribution to the festiveness of the evening suddenly seemed a pretty poor effort in comparison to hers. Barely able to restrain myself long enough to let her finish releasing me, I resumed my travels south, fingers sliding beneath the bottom edge of her dress to seek out the barely hidden areas beneath, discovering the presence of underwear even more microscopically engineered than the dress. It only marginally covered the essentials. Oh so easy to slip aside that strip of silky nothingness and move beyond.

Fixated as I now was, Juliet had other plans. Firmly manoeuvring me until I was laid back on the sofa, she slid herself down to kneel between my legs, sliding my jeans low enough to finally spot Rudolph smiling up at her from my lap. She did acknowledge him with a little smile before removing him from the equation too and setting to work on raising my Christmas spirit even further. My bliss was complete when during that indulgence she proceeded to deep-throat me, that rare and most insanely pleasing of talents, a gift that perfectly satisfied most of my Christmas wishes in one go.

It was a torturous decision to fend off the almost automatic result of such attention but I was already suspecting that we had a long night ahead of us and I thought it prudent to keep as much as possible in reserve, thinking that we would have plenty of time to revisit this position later. So, I withdrew and moved her over to lie beside the fireplace where I took my time exploring all around the edges of that slinky little Santa dress, savouring every minute of my belated Christmas.

Oral sex is one of my absolute favourite pastimes, whether giving or receiving, and I have to admit the white fluff tickling my nose as I took Little Miss Santa to the edge of the orgasmic cliff and pushed her over was definitely a festive bonus. I'm generally one for naked skin and an uncluttered view but for once, despite what promised to be a perfectly lovely body beneath, I felt inclined to leave the outfit on. I don't think I have ever found a Christmas visit from Santa more exciting or memorable.

Taking a break while Juliet lay in front of the fire, I popped to the kitchen to heat up some nibbles and open a celebratory bottle of fizz. Barely half a glass in and Little Miss Santa was raring to go again so we headed upstairs for some more fun. This time, I couldn't resist removing her seasonal trimming and, to be fair, Juliet in the flesh was every bit as fabulous as she had been when packaged. She was heavenly. What is it about a woman's skin that is so alluring? It feels so utterly different to our male skin and I find it compulsively irresistible, want to touch it, stroke it, inhale it… I covered every part of her body in this way while she lay, sighing, both of us temporarily lost, anonymously drifting in this sensory ocean, locked blissfully away from the noisy reality of the rest of the world. It enhanced my own enjoyment to hear her evident pleasure so I took my time, savouring that shared experience, before slowly, at long last, easing inside her. Juliet was a very sensuous woman and we dreamily moved through several positions, each seeming to seamlessly give way to the next without much conscious thought or apparent effort. No music on this occasion. No sound at all aside from the occasional crackle from the fireplace just audible below. Seemingly infinite dreamy enjoyment before the pace started to subtly shift upwards, one gear at time, until finally giving way to the inevitable, almost mutual surge. We lay together silently, our breathing the only sound as we floated gently back to earth. I was reluctant to move, not wanting to break too soon the contented bubble of afterglow which had descended upon us, but being a practical sort of chap it wasn't long before I'd got up to go and retrieve the nibbles and fizz. I wasn't expecting Juliet to follow me down but, before I could gather everything together, she had appeared, wearing my bathrobe, and huddled herself back on the sofa, glass in hand.

It was still only around nine o'clock, plenty of the evening left to enjoy. The drizzle had stopped now, leaving a clearing sky and hints of a bright moon in its wake, so I asked if she fancied a float in the hot tub. She was a little hesitant, evidently feeling quite cosy snuggled up by the fire and reluctant to leave it but in the end I persuaded her to give it a go. It was blissful, sipping and nibbling while we floated about in the hot bubbly water, steam rising around us, admiring the stars as they gradually appeared from behind the last of the clouds above. Before long, we'd reached the bottom of the bottle, so I sent her inside to dry off while I put the cover on the tub. Job done, I ambled in after her, feeling very relaxed and content with how the evening had gone. She wasn't in the kitchen or tucked up by the fire, where I'd expected her to be. I called up the stairs to check she was there but got no response. Not sure if she might have had enough and absconded, I went up to check, looking into my room, to be met with the sight of a naked Juliet on all fours on my bed. She turned her head to me, grinned and said 'I need you to take me down under'. I quickly gathered that she wasn't angling for a trip to Australia.

Although it didn't take long to respond to a sight or request like that, anal sex was not something I was particularly interested in or had much experienced with. At least after a good swim in the tub I knew she'd be clean, on the outside at least. She had brought plenty of lube with her and I noticed a small shiny silver vibrator on the bed next to her too as she prepared me and lubed me up, working me rapidly to a state of readiness. I wondered if I should tell her I was a novice but decided not to break the flow and just see how we got on. I

195

was naturally tentative, given the lack of experience, which actually seemed to work in the circumstances and it wasn't long before I was a good way inside. She was evidently getting a lot of pleasure out of being taken that way and I have to admit the tightness was giving me a good deal of pleasure too. She didn't seem to want me all the way in, so I'd stopped at about two thirds embedded and let her take the lead from there. It's not something I'd expected to enjoy but I was pleasantly surprised, though I'm not sure I'd actively seek it out. Once we'd settled into a gentle rhythm, I saw her reach for the dildo and immediately my radar was up again. Just when I thought I'd got to grips with new experience, another facet presented itself. She'd stopped moving now and I waited to see what she was going to do next. The sound of quiet buzzing pervaded the room as she switched it on, rubbing it through the lube before working it inside.

Oh my god!

I could feel the vibration alongside me and it had me at screaming point in no time at all. Utterly beyond my control, the release was powerful, absolute and almost instant, taking everything in my power to fight the compulsion to either thrust in or pull out. Juliet didn't take long either, squealing and convulsing, her contractions expelling the dildo with the sheer force of them and thank god, because I couldn't have taken a moment more. Ever so slowly, still in shock from the overwhelming intensity of that last manoeuvre, I eased back out of her, too dazed to say or do anything, while she collapsed forward across the bed, heaving and shuddering.

Eventually lowering myself onto the bed beside her, I re-ran the past half hour in my head while leaning back on my pillows, allowing the memory to settle on me and my shock-numbed brain to come back to life while Juliet was still sprawled across the bed, seemingly pretty comatose. It wasn't long before I felt a sip of fizz might be required so I announced my mission to Juliet's catatonic form, just in case she could hear me, and went off in search. By the time I'd fetched two fresh glasses from the kitchen and returned upstairs with them, Juliet had got herself under the covers and was showing only vague signs of being awake. I set her glass down and got into bed too, making a few conversational comments before seeing that she was unquestionably falling asleep. Fortunately, I'd got enough of a response out of her to be convinced that she was alright and in a happy place before she closed down completely. I'd offered for her to stay the night when we first arranged to meet, so she already knew she was welcome to sleep here. It wasn't long before I succumbed too.

I confessed to her the next morning that I'd been an anal virgin which she seemed to find quite amusing and a little surprising. I suppose if you were into it, then that would probably be what you would actively seek out from encounters, so to her, I guess, it was astounding that I hadn't been exposed to it or called on to perform in that way before now. It had seemed a bit of a baptism of fire to me with the vibrator in play too and I was still reeling a little from the memory of the sheer power of the resulting orgasms we'd both had. We did have another rather more standard play before getting up but it was quite gentle, though lovely and a fitting way to round off a fabulous meet.

It was, perhaps, the most unexpectedly adventurous and mutually satisfying encounter I could have wished for and perfectly timed to take the edge off the seasonal challenges. An alternative kind of Christmas, I suppose, but that year, for once, I'm quite sure I enjoyed mine every bit as much as most others enjoyed theirs, if, perhaps, in a slightly different way. We kept in touch for a while afterwards, chatting on email from time to time as we had got on so well. While we were chatting in the tub, she'd told me that her long term boyfriend had broken up with her a couple of months previously as he'd moved away with work and hadn't been able to cope with having such a long distance relationship. She'd been pretty devastated by that, apparently, and not in the mood for parties and such, hence her being available for meets while the rest of the world was out socialising or playing happy families. Shortly into the new year, she messaged me to say that the ex-boyfriend had been back in touch, evidently missing her just as much as she missed him, and she was unsure how that was going to play out but was considering moving abroad to be with him. Fairly soon after that she left the site altogether. I hope that all worked out for her and that she is in a good place. I'm still grateful to her for her fur-clad input that year and everything she did to make my Christmas the fun, happy one it had been.

Happy New Year

Alongside all the other emails I had been sending out over the previous weeks, a message had bounced into my inbox back in mid-December which turned out to be the prelude to a truly fantastic experience. The message went something along the lines of:

'Hi,

We've read your profile and verifications and think you might be just what we are looking for. We are hosting a party at home on New Year's Eve and are looking for a couple of single males... we wondered if you might be interested in meeting up for a drink to discuss what we had in mind?'

Corinne

'Absolutely', I replied, more out of curiosity than anything else.

The profile was hidden so I had no idea what to expect but after a few more message exchanges we agreed to meet at The White Swan, a pub on the main road just outside the harbour village of Bosham. It was just two weeks before Christmas and the pub was very busy. I had no idea what the couple I was meeting looked like, what age they were or anything else and I must confess that although I was intrigued I was also a little wary. I arrived at the pub half an hour early, ordered a drink and waited, watching the door slightly anxiously. Time ticked by but although people were coming and going all the while, no one gave any indication of recognition or even appeared to be looking for someone. Eventually, somewhat disappointed, I was about to finish my drink and leave when in walked a stunningly beautiful blonde woman. I mean really stunning! She was immaculately dressed, probably in her late thirties, and was closely followed by a man in his mid fifties, also very well dressed. They came straight over to me and introduced themselves, having had access to my photos so they'd been able to recognise me. We ordered some drinks and began to chat. I was, quite honestly, finding it increasingly hard to concentrate as it was obvious that Corinne's figure was every bit as tantalisingly alluring as her face. I found I needed to keep my legs pretty firmly crossed to disguise the effect she was having on me as we discussed what they were hoping this meeting might progress to. Once it had become evident that our initial discussion was heading in a mutually agreeable direction, it was decided that I would follow them back to their house where we would be able to have a more candid conversation. I followed their car for several miles and we eventually swept into the driveway of a fabulously sprawling house, which was obviously worth millions. It was beautifully and tastefully decorated and I was glad to have a few moments to myself in their large sitting room to absorb it all while they went off to the kitchen to get drinks. I was still looking around and taking everything in when Corinne reappeared carrying a tray of bottles and glasses.

She had changed into a see-through white top which revealed the red lace lingerie encasing what I later discovered were her attention-grabbing 36DD breasts. This she had teamed with a red leather mini skirt, fishnets and stilettos. Dear God! She looked absolutely incredible but it was quite an extreme look for evening drinks and left me in no doubt of the way things were heading. She sat down, enhancing my view even further. It was very, very difficult to drag my eyes away and I was now having an even harder time concealing my enthusiasm. They explained that they were intending to host a party for fourteen friends, some from the local area and some from London. Two of the guests would be single ladies, hence their desire for a couple of single men to help out with numbers. Fantastic! I was more than happy to be involved with that. So I readily agreed and she said she would be in touch with more details. She then went on to suggest she should give me a taste of what to expect at the party. Smiling suggestively at me, she sank to her knees in front of me, unzipped me and started work on a blow job I will never forget. Caught up in the moment, I reached over to caress those beautiful breasts but she stopped me en route, saying "Uh, uh, not this time, you'll have to wait for New Year's Eve for that". So I was forced to simply sit there and receive her attention without any input on my part until she had achieved her objective. Frankly, I'm quite surprised I didn't blow her bloody head off.

Tantalisingly, I then heard nothing until just a few days before the party, although, fortunately, I had all the other festive meets in the meantime to keep me occupied. I half wondered if they might have been winding me up, or whether, perhaps, the party had been called off for some reason. I was on the point of emailing to ask when a message suddenly arrived with all the details; times, directions, dress code, etc. I was quite relieved that it was going ahead as, for me, it was not only the perfect solution to New Year's Eve, a night I find a bit tricky and am unwilling to spend with 'coupley' friends, but my little warm-up session with Corrine had whet my appetite for more and I was looking forward to the possibility of exploring her further.

I arrived at around seven o'clock, as directed, along with the other single guy they'd recruited, a similarly expectant-looking black guy, Wesley. There was half an hour or so to kill before the other guests were due to arrive so the two of us grabbed a beer and got chatting, discovering that we had both received the same delightful treatment from Corinne after our respective first meets. Perhaps she was just terribly concerned about quality control but I think we both rather suspected that she was also a bit of a frisky little kitten in her own right.

Once everyone had arrived we were all introduced. As I had suspected it might be, the group seemed to be mostly made up of well-off, married couples where several of the ladies were rather younger than their husbands. The two single ladies were divorcees and both reasonably attractive. The initial stages of the party went very well with everyone mingling and chatting and a light-hearted, upbeat atmosphere. Over the next hour, the drinks continued to flow in and inhibitions began, correspondingly, to flow out of the window, giving rise to a lot of smiling, flirting and touching as the general background noise level got louder. I seemed to find myself mostly in the company of Corinne and was becoming increasingly keen for the fun to start. First, however, there was a meal, a sumptuous meal in fact, washed down with copious amounts of champagne, which gave me a little time to assess the gathering. Most of the men appeared to be in City-based jobs of the banking and finance variety, some owned their own Company, all gave the impression of wealth and all were getting increasingly rowdy and flirtatious. By the end of dinner, the atmosphere was becoming quite highly charged. As midnight approached, Corinne gathered us all outside to see some fireworks. As we watched, she silently appeared at my side and in hushed whispers told me that the next stage of the evening was imminent and that as it was her responsibility to pull names from the hat, she was jolly well going to make sure she got mine. That all sounded pretty good to me. I hoped she meant what she said.

At about half past midnight, once the last of the fireworks had whizzed and popped over our heads and all the 'Happy

New Year's' and associated snogging (which I think was just an excuse for everyone to try everyone else out for starters) was over we gathered back around the table on which was a ceramic bowl. Amongst much genial heckling and in an almost madly exuberant atmosphere by this time, Corinne, with great ceremony, organised the selecting of names by all the ladies. Having evidently removed my name from the bowl and being the last to select, Corinne did indeed end up with me. Hooray! It was announced that everyone was welcome to use any of the bedrooms or, alternatively, 'The Snug' (a smaller and less formal sitting room than the one I'd first seen) for those who preferred a group experience. In one hour a bell would be rung at which point anyone who wanted to play again with a different partner should make themselves known. She went on to say that Wesley and I would definitely be available for Round Two. Well, that was the first I'd known of that particular plan and I was glad I'd been warned that I would need to save a little something for later. I wouldn't want to disappoint anyone but I'm only human.

We were the last to move away from the table as Corinne, the perfect hostess, made sure everyone else was sorted and ensconced before abdicating from her duties. After what seemed like an eternity to a man with a bottle of fizz inside him and a major hard on, she took me off to a bedroom and finally I could go ahead and do all those things I had been aching to do for the past couple of weeks since we'd met. We kissed, briefly but passionately, before she once more dropped slowly down to the floor and, fixing my gaze like a hawk, unzipped me, managing somehow to effortlessly release me and in one impressive and accomplished move take me almost fully down her throat. I willingly let her continue to work on me for a while, taking rainy day memory snapshots in my head of the sight of her with my entirety in her mouth and that intently wicked gleam in her eyes. Close to bursting point, I had to take a deep breath, withdraw and regroup for a moment. I then took immense pleasure in finally undressing her glorious body, sliding each piece slowly off until she was completely naked before going down on her, feeling somewhat like I'd found the Holy Grail. She was fully shaven and immaculate, a couple of piercings adding interest to her pristine landscape, and I was in heaven down there. She was an absolute goddess, not one single detail disappointed me. Now urgently wanting to fuck her, I started to ease myself further up her body. Oh the joy of sliding into her, it was sublime, and she came in waves almost immediately. As she started to subside I turned her over and eased into her again. She was writhing and moaning and it took every scrap of willpower I had to force back the overwhelming desire to release but, knowing that it would likely be the end of my time with her when I came, I kept the climax at bay and I was rewarded with her taking control once more, rolling me onto my back and riding me with impassioned abandon, offering me the ultimate view as her 36DDs were shown off to their greatest advantage yet. Joyfully, I came inside her, feeling her muscles contracting down on me as she orgasmed again. We carried on moving slowly together for a few protracted moments before drifting to an eventual stop. I lay there for a while, enjoying the feeling of Corinne next to me, before she suddenly rolled over and got up in one swift move, gave me a smile as she slipped back into her underwear and then disappeared out into the hallway to ring the changeover bell.

Around half of us gathered back around the bowl in varying states of undress, including a slightly dazed-looking Wesley, who arrived being led down the hallway by his underpants at the mercy of a skinny, strident looking woman whom I'd talked to earlier. She'd given me the impression of being fairly dominant and judging by the state of him and the satisfied smirk on her face I suspected she'd given poor Wes a thorough seeing to. I was momentarily concerned that I was going to be next on her list and not sure I was quite ready yet to take that sort of pace but I was almost immediately collared by a woman who wanted me to fuck her whilst her husband watched. I confess to being slightly relieved. Fortunately, Debbie was rather attractive, if not as stunning as Corinne, and the taste and smell of an attractive woman always seems to get my engines revving again so I managed without too much difficulty to reawaken the beast just by going down on her. Glancing to the side, I could see her husband nodding off in a chair in the corner which made me chuckle to myself as I climbed aboard for my second ride of the night, taking my time and enjoying her as thoroughly as possible before yielding to the climactic urges and then falling fairly promptly into an exhausted sleep.

Waking later that morning, alone in the room and with daylight visible behind the drawn curtains, I lay contemplating the events of the night before whilst I allowed the extent of my hangover to make itself known. I came rather ponderously to two conclusions: first, that it had probably been one of the strangest but most fun New Year's Eves I'd ever had and, second, that my hangover wasn't proving nearly as vicious as it should have been. All in all, a pretty good start to a fresh new year! Cautiously, I started easing myself out of bed, observing the thinly scattered array of clothing on the floor. Barely any of it was mine and with a long sigh I had to acknowledge that I was, in fact, unsure of the whereabouts of the majority of my clothes. Fortunately, I could hear no immediate signs of movement outside so, pulling on my shirt and boxers which I'd eventually found thrown on a chair, I stumbled out onto the landing to see if I could locate the remainder as well as my overnight bag. I found the bag without too much difficulty, managed to find a bathroom after tentatively trying a couple of doors and ten minutes later was feeling reasonably presentable.

Standing, at least now fully clothed, on the spacious landing, I considered two doors on the corridor, trying hopelessly to recall which one I'd been taken through by Corinne, that being the room in which I would, no doubt, find the remainder of my absent attire, although, potentially a good deal else I might not necessarily want to see. After some moments of contemplation I decided not to risk it and headed downstairs from which direction I could hear faint chatter and detect the welcome smell of coffee and breakfast. There were a few people congregated in the kitchen, some looking in decidedly better shape than others, and the beginnings of a supply of cooked breakfast was apparently imminent. Corinne was evidently fully back in hostess mode. I greeted everyone, helped myself to coffee and eased into a chair, suddenly ravenous. Over the next half hour or so, more people drifted in from wherever they'd ended up after last night's revelry to be similarly propped up with bacon, croissants and caffeine. There was no sign of Debbie but her husband put in an appearance after about ten minutes, along with a shambolic looking Wesley. He seemed exhausted. I got the impression he'd been quite popular with the ladies and, by the look of him, had probably been driven to the outer limits of human endurance.

'You OK mate?' I asked him, quietly.

'All good... all good....' was all he seemed to be able to get out in subdued reply. I couldn't decide if he was in shock or just monumentally hungover. I gave him a knowing look, getting a sheepish grin in return. I think we'd both had a brilliant night.

Feeling fortified, I headed back upstairs to continue the search for my dinner suit, tie and shoes, which I eventually spotted through the now open door of one of the rooms upstairs. There was a woman in the room, seemingly asleep and lying face down in the bed, so I tiptoed around, trying not to disturb her as I picked up my things. Hearing movement from the bed as I bent to pick up my shoes, I glanced across to find her half turned to face me. It was Debbie. "Morning' I said, as she squinted at me through one, barely open, eye. She made no response but continued vaguely trying to focus. 'You OK? Would you like some coffee?' I volunteered, not really sure what to say next. She blinked her half open eye but otherwise just continued to lay there. 'I think I'll get you some coffee' I said and left the room, returning a few minutes later only to find her returned to her original position and, apparently, in a mild coma. I set the coffee down on the side and left her to it.

I eventually left at around eleven thirty, after thanking my hosts and saying goodbye to the remaining guests. Wesley, who opted to leave at the same time, walked out with me and we had a brief chat as we went. He confirmed my suspicions that he'd had quite a demanding night, ending up fielding three full sessions with different women. Heroic effort! No wonder he'd looked so wasted. I felt a mixture of awe at his stamina and relief that I'd been spared an additional session.

I'd have loved to get together with Corinne again but, despite exchanging a few post-party emails, we haven't arranged another meet. Ah well, I was very glad to have been involved in their interesting little gathering and it had been a fantastic way to survive the transition into the new year

David B

RESPECT

My next meet was with a couple, Mike and Lindsay, whose profile had appeared during the first day or two of January. They implied that they were fairly new to swinging, which perhaps explained the lack of verifications, but overall they had seemed nice and I thought I'd give them a try. They replied to my message, seeming friendly and fairly keen and after a couple of emails we arranged to meet and had a pleasant enough time chatting for an hour or so.

On the face of it, things seemed to be going pretty well but although Mike was certainly interactive, a little loud even, Lindsay was giving me the impression of being a bit tense and wasn't contributing much to the conversation. That wasn't particularly unusual for the start of a meet, however, and as they were also newbies I didn't focus overly much on it, expecting her to relax over the course of a drink or two. An hour later and Mike had become almost overbearingly loud while Lindsay, though looking visibly less tense than she had been, still did not seem convinced. It was fairly quiet in the bar, which I supposed wouldn't be helping her to feel confident about speaking up if she had reservations about anything, whether that was to do with me personally or about the situation per se. So I thought I'd open up the field a bit and try to find out what was going on. I suggested to them that it might be more conducive to move on to my house where we could have another drink in a more relaxed setting and then left them alone to discuss this for a few minutes. When I returned, I found them apparently both keen to come round to the house straight away so we finished our drinks and headed out.

The atmosphere relaxed once we were on my sofa with a bottle of wine on the table before us. I tried gently flirting with Lindsay but she still seemed a bit reticent. As we chatted, it became apparent that although Lindsay was indeed new to the scene, Mike was quite a seasoned swinger having indulged on numerous occasions with previous partners. As the evening went on, without putting Lindsay on the spot by questioning her directly, I tried to engineer the conversation in ways which would help me confirm my impression that she was being either coerced, or very strongly encouraged, into this scenario somewhat against her will. They left after about an hour and a half and it was all perfectly friendly but, despite my subtle attempts to delve beneath the surface, I actually had no idea what Lindsay was really thinking, despite knowing probably way more than I needed to about Mike's opinions and predilections. I had a text from them that same evening requesting a meet and play. I considered this for a while and decided, on balance, to decline. Although I had found Lindsay lovely company and, actually, very attractive I had no desire to get involved in a scenario where anyone was possibly being put into a situation they didn't want whole-heartedly to be in.

I suppose I could have invited them over and let Lindsay set the pace but aside from my suspicion that Mike's oppressive manner would make it difficult to read Lindsay's lead easily, if she hadn't seemed keen in her own right I would then have had to call a halt and abort the meet which would have been awkward and could potentially have caused problems between them. I was uncomfortable enough with the thought of having to do something like that to be quite prepared to chalk it up to an enjoyable evening's company and leave it there.

I messaged them back, politely declining, without giving specific reasons. I just told them I had reservations about proceeding but wished them well. I see the profile is still on the site and there are new verifications so perhaps Lindsay has been won over and is now happily integrated or possibly Mike has found himself a more enthusiastic partner to share his encounters with and slotted her into Lindsay's place. Either way, I have no regrets about sidestepping that one. I just didn't want to be party to something I felt so dubious about.

Spanish Eyes

Also in early January, another new profile appeared on the site and immediately caught my eye. It was put up by a couple who were apparently brand new to swinging but their profile seemed very upbeat, fresh and uncomplicated so I sent them a cheery, welcoming message. I later found out that they'd had nearly a hundred responses to their profile in the first week of it going live. That's a lot of choice so I was amazed and pretty flattered that with all of those options they had bothered to respond to me. My ever growing list of verifications had apparently swung their decision in my favour.

We arranged to have our initial meet at the Deer's Hut pub in Liphook. I made sure I was there fairly early and set myself up, as usual, in a corner of the bar with a beer and a good view of the door. The only picture I had seen was a body shot of Lara which Matt had sent me early on in our discussions. It had certainly captured my interest at the time as it looked like the body of a page three model. I know from experience that the face does not always match the allure of the body (and vice versa) so my expectations were held in check but, having seen that picture, I felt pretty certain I would be able to overlook the face if that was necessary. I was aware that Lara was Spanish and that Matt was Italian so I thought they might be easy enough to spot, even without having seen head shots.

When they came through the door my jaw nearly hit the table and all I could think was 'oh please, please let that be them'. Lara was stunning. I mean proper, drop-dead gorgeous, model stunning. Tall and slender with spectacular blue eyes, set off by long, thick waves of dark, sheeny hair. A chest of almost unfeasible proportion for a woman of her build stood proud above a tiny waist and perfect legs. I was dumbstruck. Frankly, it was all I could do to gather my senses enough to string a coherent sentence together in time to greet them. I could hardly believe my eyes or my luck and was determined to do everything in my power not to put them off. I knew they had never engaged in a threesome, never even swung before and that Matt was likely to be a bit sensitive to the thought of someone else enjoying his wife in that way, so I trod very carefully through our discussions.

Happily, the evening went really well and after a couple of drinks and some fairly lively conversation I tentatively suggested that they pop home with me for a glass of wine, just to see where I lived and assess whether they thought it would be suitable place to have a second meet if they wanted one. As I had hoped, they took to the idea and were soon ensconced on my sofa, glasses in hand, while I set about lighting a fire, occasionally taking a surreptitious look at Lara. She obviously had the time and money available to keep herself in perfect shape and, having clicked so easily with her too, I was, by this time, more than a little excited about the prospect of getting intimately acquainted. Matt fitted a familiar profile: rather older than his wife, slightly out of shape and evidently very well off. A classic situation which I'd encountered a number of times now, where the wealthy man has acquired himself a suitably stunning young wife whom he eventually fails to be able to service and so settles on this option in preference to losing her altogether. Perhaps it feels, to those husbands, as though they haven't completely lost control if they can be involved in the solution at least to this level.

Lara divulged that they had been married since she was twenty-one and that if things progressed with this arrangement I would be only the third person she had ever slept with, a concept which astounded me given that she was such a stunning and engaging woman. Matt had, over the years, slowly become almost completely impotent and Lara's frustration was now undeniable, hence them deciding to try this route as a way to relieve that without breaking the relationship up. I put them at their ease about their choice by explaining that this was a common situation and that I had met a number of couples who found that this particular solution worked very well for them. I think they were convinced because from that point on they started discussing the next meet as if it was a foregone conclusion. Obviously, I wasn't going to argue as that was just fine with me, and we arranged a date for the following week as they now seemed increasingly keen to move things along and get started.

On the night, they showed up at about eight thirty and I welcomed them in having taken extra care to set the scene as well as I could. We opened a bottle and the first glass was poured, although Lara immediately confessed she'd already had a drink before they'd left home in an attempt to soothe her nerves. Although she certainly didn't seem drunk, a hint of something in her eyes made me suspect she might have had more than just the one. They sat on the sofa while I perched on the chair and as we chatted over the course of a glass or two they appeared to settle into the situation in their own ways. Matt sank back into the sofa, looking calm and relaxed, while Lara become very animated and increasingly flirtatious. As we were getting to the end of the second glass, the conversation turned to playtime and I suggested they might like to take their wine upstairs so Matt could help Lara to get undressed before I came up to join them. They seemed happy with that, relieved even, especially Matt, which was good as I certainly didn't want him suddenly getting the jitters and calling it all off at this critical moment. That would have been exceedingly sad and not a little frustrating with the prospect of exploring Lara's exotically perfect landscape now so close at hand. So they made their way upstairs and I said I would join them in a few minutes. I could hear them talking in low voices but they sounded pretty content so I started heading up the stairs. I opened the door slowly, having already undressed and lubed myself up, just in case. I wanted as little of this process as possible to go in on front of Matt, fearing that it might cause him to change his mind.

I took in the vision of an enticingly naked Lara, standing, as she was, next to a partially undressed Matt. They looked so incongruous together; he in his socks and shirt, she looking like she'd just stepped off the set of some glamourous porn movie. I smiled at her but, rather gratifyingly, she didn't seem to notice, her gaze fixed steadfastly on my already engorged cock.

'Oh my god' she said, 'what the hell do you feed that on?'

Well, there aren't many things you could say to a man which would please him more. I wasn't sure what she had to compare it to, but I took the compliment anyway, in fact I think he probably even grew a little bit more in sheer pride. During our conversations earlier that evening, Lara had divulged that she desperately needed fucking, long and hard, and that she also quite liked the idea of being dominated a little. Hoping I wasn't about to push Matt's boundaries too far, I stepped over to Lara's side and picked her up. She was a good five feet eight tall but slender as a reed and, as I suspected, weighed virtually nothing. She appeared slightly startled, her eyes wide, but didn't resist, letting me carry her the few steps to the bed where I placed her down. I could feel her body physically quivering. It was electrifying to have this staggeringly beautiful woman reclining on my bed trembling with eagerness. It felt like there were fireworks going off in my brain, my skin was quite literally prickling with anticipation. As she lay there, I raised her arms above her head and placed her fingers round the wooden slats of the headboard behind her, closing them tight. 'Don't let go' I said firmly, looking straight into her wide blue eyes.

She looked back at me in such a way I thought she might actually come before we'd even started. Fixing her gaze with my own, I ran my hands gently down over her body, relishing the feel of her perfect skin under my fingers, still unable to believe I was being let loose on this ravishing creature. I traced the tantalising curves of her hips and thighs, feeling her pent-up tension rippling into the tips of my fingers, before trailing my hands up to her incredible, heart-stoppingly beautiful breasts, lingering there as long as I dared. They were simply magnificent. Spellbinding. Honestly, I could have spent an entire night in contentedly blissful worship of their glorious perfection. Almost reluctant to move on I had to force myself to shift my attention further south, dragging my hands away and sending them steadily on down over her perfectly trimmed bush to slip between her legs prising them apart. Easing onto the bed, I knelt between them spreading them wider with my knees. I was suddenly tempted to twang myself at her, wanting to feel myself slap, repeatedly, hard against that manicured bush, but, although I had kept Matt firmly out of my focus, he was still there in my peripheral vision and I reminded myself that excess playfulness might well prove counter-productive. So I contented myself with a little gentle and discreet teasing of her clit with the tip of my cock until she was moaning and arching. I straightened out, hovering above her, then slowly lowered myself down, before plunging in fairly hard, the lube now most definitely surplus to requirements. She came almost immediately, writhing and bucking though I noticed she kept her hands still locked tight to the slats where I'd placed them. To be fair, I was quite amazed she'd lasted as long as she did. I've never felt such tension and anticipation in a woman, it was like playing with an electric fence, knowing what will happen the moment you touch it. As the waves continued to flood over her she wrapped her legs tight around me, drawing me

215

determinedly into her. 'Harder', she breathed, and I obliged, losing myself in a deep, strong rhythm while she let her legs drop to the bed, knees bent, head thrown back.

Absorbed as I was in the divinely intense experience of Lara in full flight, I had completely forgotten about Matt but was suddenly reminded of his presence when, without warning, a camera lens appeared between my legs, just visible between thrusts. Momentarily resenting this intrusion, I quickly reminded myself that I was, after all, fucking his luscious wife and he was probably therefore within his rights to want a memento so I did my best to ignore him. He was obviously a big fan of the close up though and also of the creative angle, sometimes getting so close I started to fear that he might cause some physical damage to one or other of us. Eventually my patience failed me.

'Hey Spielberg,' I said, trying to keep it friendly, 'I'm fine with the filming but could you do me a favour and just back off a bit?' He was apologetic and retreated immediately, leaving me to regain my focus which I did by sucking mercilessly on Lara's enormous, though not quite all natural breasts. Almost instantly, the camera returned, so close to mouth and nipple I'm surprised it didn't chip a tooth or administer a black eye.

'For god's sake man!' I said, this time giving him a bit of a look.

He seemed to get the message and backed off once more but evidently Lara resented the intrusion even more than I did because she immediately gave vent to a torrent of what sounded like pretty harsh abuse, in Spanish, her words rolling out in a powerful and expanding wave, which positively reverberated off the walls. To be honest I am quite turned on by foreign languages and accents so there was a brief period where I found the sound of her quite erotic. Sadly, though, she wound herself into such a frenzy she rather lost concentration on what we were doing. This was made worse when Matt retorted with an outburst of his own and soon the pair of them were having such a row I reluctantly had to give the mission up as a lost cause and dismount. They were so engrossed they barely noticed. Leaving them to it, I went off downstairs, got dressed, grabbed a drink and sat waiting for them to reappear. I could still hear them yelling away at one another for some time before the volume started to drop and then came abruptly to a stop. A few minutes later they came downstairs, fully dressed and looking rather sheepish. Matt went off to get their coats while Lara stayed and apologised for the way things had ended up.

Apparently, Matt had become jealous. Predicting in advance that this might happen, they had fixed on the idea of him having a camera so that he could distract himself by taking shots. The extreme closeness of the shots was apparently a measure of the extreme jealousy he had been experiencing, which is what they'd been shouting at each other about. I dismissed it and told her not to worry, letting her know that I was open to setting up another meet if they decided they wanted to try again but she shook her head and said she doubted Matt was going to get his head around this one. The very next day their profile disappeared from the site and I've had no further contact with either of them since. I was a little disappointed as I would very much have liked to have another session with Lara but it was not to be.

Ah well, plenty of fish still left in the big blue swinging sea.

David B

Wake Me Up Before You Go

I was active on numerous websites by now, some of which had been free to join and some of which were fee-paying. A couple of those sites were proving more fruitful than others. I find I get less interaction and definitely a lower 'conversion rate' from the free websites. Perhaps that's because more people who actually start to pursue the lifestyle properly and want better quality prospects use the paying sites, or eventually migrate there from the free ones once they've tried it out and realise the pitfalls. There was one site, a free one, which I had kept an profile on although I hadn't had any real interaction with anyone from it. However, idly flicking through it one day for want of anything better to do, I saw a profile that did catch my interest, posted by a woman who lived fairly nearby. She was also single which, after my recent encounter with Lara and Matt, sounded appealingly uncomplicated. I sent her an introductory message without any great expectations but she surprised me by replying the very next day. We exchanged a few more emails over the following day or two before going on to arrange a preliminary meet at the Earl of March in Lavant just a couple of days later.

The evening went really well. Teresa was a pleasant looking brunette, slim and sparkly-eyed, although, within a fairly short time of meeting her, I suspected that was as much to do with her anxiety levels as anything else. She just seemed like one of those people who tread nervously through life waiting for the next bomb to drop. She was animated and entertaining company, however. We laughed and chatted and got on well; it was actually, by any standards, a great evening and we parted at the end saying we would definitely get together again. I was quite surprised, then, to get a text from her the next morning saying that she was 'in a bad place at the moment' and that she didn't want to take things any further for now. I was a little disappointed as she had been lovely, but I simply returned a text saying that of course that was fine, I completely understood and hoped she got herself into a better place soon. Despite having had a fun evening, it just proved that you can't always tell what someone is thinking, whether there is enough attraction on their part or where they might be emotionally.

No great issue though, these things happen and I really thought no more about it. So I was pleasantly surprised when, about three weeks later, a text appeared from her asking if I'd be up for another meet.

'Abso-bloody-lutely!' I replied and invited her to come for dinner at mine with the option to stay over if she wanted to so she didn't have to worry about driving. She said straight away that she'd love to stay over, which I hadn't expected after the slightly hit and miss start, but I was pleased as it opens out the time available so much and takes that pressure off. She was now, apparently, very keen to move things along and so we set a date for that coming weekend. My little cottage is a perfect place for putting people at their ease, I find, and Teresa settled in very quickly after she arrived. I'd put a couple of bottles of fizz on ice and she was very happy to get stuck into those. Soon we were laughing and joking, just as we had been in the pub on that first evening, with a fair bit of suggestive chat thrown in. It can be great when you have that extra bit of time before things get started, an opportunity to build things up more slowly, prolong the anticipation. Especially when you know what lies ahead, it can be very titillating and a bit of rapport helps the whole process along no end. I'd been a bit concerned that Teresa might still be 'in a bad place' and back off when it came down to it but I needn't have worried. She was plainly good to go and in great spirits, very touchy-feely and flirtatious.

We laughed and teased our way through dinner, by the end of which, it seemed, neither of us could wait to get started on dessert which began with Teresa giving me blow job from under the table with her mouth full of Prosecco. That was a new experience for me. The tingle and sudden changes in temperature enhanced the much tried and tested theme in ways I couldn't believe I hadn't thought of before, certainly well worth the investment in the fizz. Not surprisingly, that totally broke the ice and we were soon both semi-naked and romping about in the kitchen in the early stages of foreplay. She was quite frisky and I found myself bending her over the butcher's block and 'spanking' her for being so naughty, pausing between spanks to run my hand down between her legs, briefly exploring before withdrawing for the next round of 'punishment'. Gradually, that seemed to bring her down from her slightly hyperactive mode to a more sexually focused level and slowly the spanking gave way to more of the fondling until she dropped her forehead down to the block and began to push gently back against my hand, now concentrating fully on what I was doing to her. She was, by now, naked aside from panties which I slid down over her hips, letting them drop to the floor where she kicked them aside, widening her stance as she did so. I continued to stroke and caress her, feeling her wetness, penetrating her with fingers before moving up behind her. Her head was still resting against the wooden surface, arms reaching up and out to the sides where her hands clung to the edges. She was breathing deeply and had barely moved since things had reached this level, though there was more than enough verbal response to my probing to convince me she was enjoying it. Holding her by the hips, I drew her back towards me, tip gently gliding back and forth between her legs, teasing yet more juices from her, using my hand to push myself flat against her, still not penetrating but applying more pressure as she squirmed against me, before finally easing in to her full length, the relief palpable for both of us. Suddenly, raising herself up on her arms, she lifted her head and thrust back hard against me.

Caught up with the sudden change in energy, I went with it, pounding into her, hands tight on her hips, driving harder. She was making deep, rolling sounds now, her pace gradually slowing just a little, though just as forceful, seeming to want to take me ever deeper, her back arched, head back, the length of her hair almost touching the cleft between her cheeks. Moments later her head dropped forward once more, vocal sounds ceased and were replaced with deep, heavy breathing. I kept moving, waiting to feel the tell-tale tensing within her as she came. She left me hanging, however. No climax materialised, instead she pulled away, turned and, without a word, led me towards the stairs. Relieved, as I'd thought for a moment she might have had enough already, I followed her up, shepherding her into my room where she all but threw me on the bed, straddling me and impaling herself once more. She was quite a forceful girl in her way, but I was happy to throw myself upon her mercy, I don't think there would have been much she could have done to me that I wouldn't have eagerly welcomed.

Now dominant and obviously enjoying being in control, she rode me with all the passion of a rodeo cowgirl, a wild look in her eye that made me glad she wasn't wearing spurs. She leaned forward on my wrists, pinning me down while she continued to abuse me, hard and fast, driving me to distraction and eventually drawing an explosion from me which I couldn't have held back if I'd tried. She kept right on moving through it too, until I couldn't take any more and was forced to make moves to ease her pace. Only then did she concede and release, grinding down on me as she came in dramatic, torturous spasms before pulling away and collapsing beside me. I'm not sure if she slept immediately too but, for me, the post-coital close-down overtook me in minutes and I must have slept for an hour or so before I came to with a jolt, realising all the lights were still on. It was around half past midnight but Teresa appeared to be fast asleep beside me so I crept out of the room and downstairs to switch lights off and make sure all was secure before returning and, finding Teresa still out for the count, going back to sleep.

I was rudely, but not unwelcomely, awakened the following morning by the sensation of Teresa's arm resting on my waist while her hand was working gently away at the already-present morning glory. As wake up calls go, that was a pretty good one and, happily accepting this new scenario, I lay back and continued to drift along as I gradually lifted out of the sleepy depths. I was in no great hurry to wake as it still felt (and in fact was) pretty early but my lack of urgency didn't deter her. Before I'd even fully come round, her enthusiasm had got the better of her, she'd climbed on top of me, guided me in, and we were off again, rocking away as the spring morning light grew brighter, just for the sheer pleasure of it.

What a great way to start the day! A rather shorter session this time but after the previous nights monumentally energetic input it was entirely satisfactory, perhaps even something of a relief. Once we'd finished with each other, I jokingly chided her for being so forward as to take advantage of me in my sleep. She just giggled and said she'd woken to the sight of my flagpole pointing at the sky and it would have seemed rude to ignore it. I suppose she had a fair point there. I went off and made coffee which we lay in bed sipping while we chatted away, comfortable and relaxed, until she decided she had to get going. I must say I was quite sad to see her leave when she eventually headed off home around mid-morning. She was easy to be with, great to talk to and I could quite happily have spent the rest of the day with her, chatting and romping.

I sent her a couple of messages, one straight afterwards thanking her for coming over and for being such terrific company and one a week or so later, but had no response and have heard nothing since. That was fine, of course. Again, that's the deal, no strings, no obligations, but she was a lovely, vivacious girl and it would have been good to know that she was alright even if she didn't want to continue to stay in touch. I've taught myself to assume that no news is good news. She'd certainly seemed happy enough when she left.

David B

Fat Bottom Gal

Having had a great time with Teresa, I took a closer look at the website I'd seen her details on and saw another profile there which I'd missed before. It had been set up by a single girl who lived a little further west down the coast but not a million miles from me. Trudie's profile had some nice pictures up, nothing particularly erotic, just standard, decent pictures and it all looked very good. I lost no time in getting in touch and after a few exchanges of email we agreed to meet up at pub on the edge of Portsmouth.

I'd like to think I'm pretty open minded, not particularly judgemental and generally forgiving but I'd been caught out a few times and was beginning to get a bit fed up with it. When Trudie appeared I was immediately struck by her physical presence, but not in a good way. Now, genuinely, I find most women's shapes and sizes appealing and, on balance, quite favour a fuller figure. But I don't like to be lied to or mislead and then expected to just accept it because I'm too polite to tell it like it is or risk being thought rude.

In this case, the plain and simple fact of the matter was that Trudie, who, granted, did have a very pretty face, had the most EMORMOUS arse I've ever seen. You'll be thinking I'm a fussy bugger, I expect, or perhaps you'll have in mind a larger behind of the 'celebrity' type which you might well find very appealing, but I promise I am talking extreme here. This was not an arse which could attribute its size to generous womanly curves, which I love and admire, this was an arse of such extraordinary shape and dimension that I suspect she could have earned a living from exhibiting it as a novelty spectacle. I daresay there are plenty of guys out there who would find the sight of it erotic and that's what gets me annoyed. If she had been more honest about it on her profile I expect she'd get plenty of offers from guys, all of whom would know what to expect and were there because they liked it. Just because I swing, it doesn't mean I'll cheerfully fuck anything that moves regardless of whether I like the sight of it or not. On most of the previous occasions when similar situations have occurred, I've been too polite to say anything, just got through a drink or whatever the immediate situation has thrown at me and taken my leave at the earliest opportunity which I felt wouldn't cause offence, but this time I couldn't let it go.

Moderating my voice and comments, as I certainly didn't intend or want to be nasty, I explained to her that I felt she'd got me there under false pretences, that her photos, although gorgeous, were clearly several years out of date and that she was, in fact, overweight and a fairly unique shape with it (just in case she was genuinely in denial of the reality) and that she ought to be honest with herself and others about that.

She was not happy.

I can see why this situation had not made her happy and it hadn't given me any pleasure to be the one who had caused her not to be happy either, but I still felt pretty riled.

After I'd said my piece there was, naturally enough, an air of, well, let's call it awkwardness. There didn't seem much else to say nor really any way to salvage anything worthwhile from the evening so after a few minutes I left, paying the bill for the unfinished drinks on my way out.

I did check some time later but, of course, she hadn't amended her profile at all and in fact, I later saw, had gone on to put up an identical profile on another site so my words and actions obviously had no impact. Perhaps she was honestly in denial and couldn't see beyond the photos of her much less curvy former self, which she continued to use. Perhaps my response was not in line with most other guys and she normally had no negative reactions. Or, perhaps she had done some extreme dieting and the photos were now more representative, but I suspect not.

It's an interesting exercise in observation to meet someone for the first time when you've only had access to a profile they've created by themselves, about themselves, as anyone who has tried internet dating of any description will know. People's profiles, naturally I suppose, most often resemble the person they would like to be, or, sometimes, the person they think you will want them to be, far more than representing the reality. The anomalies can be huge but it often reveals a lot about the mind of the person you're dealing with.

Happy Campers

As we headed on into summer, I spotted a profile put up by Bob and Karen, a couple who had listed themselves as based in the New Forest. It had a nice, chilled tone and plenty of verifications. Definitely worth a try, so I got in touch and they replied suggesting that we start by having a chat on the phone. It was a slightly unusual way to begin the process but I went along with it and we managed to organise a three-way conversation that went along easily enough, with lots of joking and banter, and ended with us arranging to meet at a pub, the Three Legged Cross, in Verwood the following Friday night.

We had seen photos of each other so I knew that Karen was fairly attractive and a buxom lass, but to say she had dressed provocatively would be a bit of an understatement. During our chat on the phone I had admitted to being something of a 'breast man' and she had laughed and made a couple of quips, but perhaps she had remembered that comment because her low cut top was tantalisingly revealing and seemed to have been purposely chosen to torture a man with my preferences. She had a cleavage to die for, full, deep and bouncy. I was all but licking my lips at the sight, fighting off an overwhelming desire to lean forward and just bury my face in them there and then. To any ladies reading this, please forgive us guys for having these feelings, it's in-built by nature and I think we are all, to one degree or another, at its mercy.

It was an almighty challenge to lift my gaze the required forty or so degrees to make eye contact, but with superhuman effort I managed it eventually to find her twinkling at me, an amused smile on her lips. She was a good looking woman too, not in an obvious way but she had a self-assured sexual confidence that could easily draw you in. An aura, if you will. So it was not just me whose attention was caught by the sight of her and her perfectly displayed kahunas. On several occasions I spotted other pairs of eyes which had been magnetically drawn to the sight of those bobbling beauties. Karen appeared oblivious to the attention but when I made some subtle reference to it she gave me a sidelong look and winked. She knew exactly what effect she was having. She was quite a saucy bird, was Karen, very quick with the flirtatious banter, and the three of us had a great evening. It turned out that they actually lived elsewhere but they kept a caravan at a site in the new forest area, which they used as a base for most of their swinging encounters. They invited me back there for some fun and although the last meet I'd agreed to which had involved a caravan-based get together hadn't been too inspiring, that didn't stop me agreeing to go back with Bob and Karen to theirs. As caravans go, it was quite modern and nice. There is something about the thought of caravans which conjures up a slightly seedy feeling for me but sitting comfortably with a glass of wine in my hand, soaking up the hint of a holiday atmosphere, this one was really quite pleasant. It didn't take long to get down to business though, as we'd had plenty of preamble at the pub. Karen started to undress in her entertainingly saucy way whilst Bob and I sat smiling and sipping as we watched, giving way to more verbal encouragement as she teased us with her slowly increasing nakedness.

Down to just her underwear, she picked up her glass and leaned against the bedroom door frame. She was curvy and voluptuous, just oozing cheeky sex appeal. She gave me a wicked, come-hither smile and I felt myself jump to attention like she'd just sent me a psychic electric shock. God, this woman was actually pretty hot. Slinking her way over to me, she leaned in and unbuttoned my shirt, spreading it open before straddling me and then slowly, tantalisingly, removing her bra, bringing her liberated breasts towards my face. Cradling them in my hands, loving the feel of their plump fullness, I brought them forward the rest of the way and let my lips and tongue finally do what they'd been aching to do all evening. Reaching down, she started to unbutton my jeans, though with some difficulty, as I was firmly fixed, by hand and mouth, to her succulent breasts, reluctant to release them in the slightest way from my clutches. Chuckling, she managed to withdraw from my rapt attention and dropped to her knees between my legs where she buried her head in my lap and started to work along my length with tongue and lips, suddenly languorous and sensual. Bob sat a few feet away on the next bench casually watching, seemingly enjoying the view in a laid-back, benevolent kind of way. Happy that we weren't going to be hindered by his presence, I turned my full attention back to Karen and allowed myself to be towed along on the tide. She detached herself while she removed my jeans and shirt, then took me off to the little bedroom area where she laid herself provocatively on the bed, giving me a mischievous smile while her hand glided smoothly over her clean-shaven pussy.

As an aside, I have only occasionally seen even minimal signs of lady-bush on my swinging travels. I don't know if that's just a 'thing' now for most women everywhere or if it is more prevalent in swinging circles as I only have my encounters to go on. Whilst I'm not a massive fan of a rumble in an out-and-out jungle, I'm not at all averse to a well-maintained lady-garden. That said, I have nothing against the clean-shaven trend either. At first I had a few questions in my head about it, after all, I like women, not little girls, but I adjusted pretty quickly and concluded that when it comes to coiffed versus coote, in the right circumstances, I am happy to bury my face in either!

Whilst Karen reclined in her state of idle play, I removed the last of my clothes and climbed onto the bed with her, indulging myself for a time once more with her gorgeous breasts before turning on all fours and lowering myself into her mouth as I buried my head between her legs where I paid her adorably naked lady-piece the attention it deserved. The confined space of that little room had the potential to be a little claustrophobia-inducing but in fact I found I quite liked its slightly cave-like ambience in this context. Sensing Karen's excitement building, I turned her over, spreading her legs far apart, opening that beautiful, inviting pussy wide before diving in. We stayed in that position for quite a long time, rocking back and forth, for my part just lost in a haze of pleasure, before I turned her back to face me, taking as much of her right breast and nipple into my mouth as I could get, feasting on it like a starved infant while I ploughed deep into her. She was moaning and trembling then suddenly cried out as she came hard, gripping my shoulders with her fingernails, almost to the point of breaking the skin.

Caught in the moment I withdrew and, moments later, spurted over those gargantuan breasts, leaving a satisfying trail over them both. After a brief respite to catch my breath, I began looking around for something to clean her up with and became aware of Bob standing in the doorway, watching, a professional-looking camera in his hand. He knelt on the floor and leaned over the bed, taking close ups of the glistening beads on Karen's breasts. Apparently, they liked to keep mementoes of their encounters! Bob took a lot of pride in his photographic efforts and, seeing as he was naked by this time too, it was clear he was getting a fair bit of pleasure out of it. Once he'd finished and had retreated for a moment to put the camera back in its case, I took the opportunity to smooth away my residues with Kleenex, getting another shiver of erotic pleasure out of manipulating Karen's cleavage one more time. Bob returned almost immediately and it was obvious he was intending to take his turn with Karen. I wasn't sure I felt entirely comfortable with sitting and watching in such a tiny space and started preparing to get myself out of the way. It was going to be a bit of a job simply getting to the door without climbing over the other two though, which would have been a bit awkward as Bob had already turned Karen over and was lining himself up for entry. However, the decision was taken out of my hands. when she reached over and pulled me towards her, clamping her lips around me and leaving me with no further option, or in fact desire, to escape. She had some stamina that woman and it was well into the early hours by the time we'd finished.

Despite the time, Bob announced that he was intending to drive Karen and himself home that night, as they had to be at a function the next day. They gave me the option to stay the rest of the night in their caravan, an offer I gratefully accepted, so they departed, leaving me with instructions for securing everything when I left, and I slept peacefully for the rest of the night before heading off in the morning. They also asked me if I'd like to join them again the following Friday for another session. I'd actually had a great night so I agreed, thinking it would be nice to have an easy play date sitting in the diary.

When I arrived the following week, slightly late after battling the Friday evening traffic on the A27, I found they'd ordered a takeaway and there was dinner waiting. Very civilised, I thought. We had a good chat and catch up over dinner and I was struck by how normal this sort of situation was starting to feel, chatting like old friends with people I had known such a short time but already had carnal knowledge of. In some ways it was a bit odd when you thought about it like that, but I did feel particularly comfortable with these two. When we'd finished eating, I saw a look pass between them and a subtle nod from Karen. I gave them an enquiring look, wondering what was coming next. They both grinned and went on to tell me that they were regular attendees at Swinger's Caravan Club meets and there was one happening nearby the following weekend. They offered to take me along and introduce me if I wanted to join them. This was a whole new concept to me and my interest was immediately sparked. They filled me in on the general format and details and I quickly decided it was something that I definitely wanted to experience at least once. After dinner Karen and I went off to the bedroom and had a play but it was relatively short and sweet compared with the previous time and was peppered with conversation about the upcoming meet. I was very intrigued by the idea of camping with a whole group of swinging-minded individuals. It all sounded full of possibility and a very nice way to spend a weekend, I thought, although, in the back of my mind, part of the appeal was that it sounded like an easy thing to quietly walk away from if I got there and found that I didn't like it after all.

They had given me instructions and a phone number to contact to book myself a caravan in the right place so I was on the phone first thing the next morning to organise that straight away. I was actually really looking forward to it and I thought the week would probably drag by as a consequence, but in fact it flew past and by lunchtime on Saturday I had driven to the campsite and was installed in the caravan which would be mine for the weekend. I had a good look around and made myself at home, then poured myself a glass of wine and took up a position outside in the sunshine, from where I could get a view of others turning up and assess the situation as it unfolded. It was a warm day, perfectly pleasant for relaxing with some vino. Over the following few hours between twenty and thirty vehicles drew up, everything from VW Campers to fancy new motorhomes, and an array of people stepped out covering a surprisingly wide age spectrum from a couple in their twenties to couples in their sixties. I believe there was only one other single person there, a woman, but suffice to say, not quite my cup of tea. Once Bob and Karen had arrived and sorted themselves out, I wandered over and we sat together with a bottle of wine enjoying the buzz around us as people began to wander the site, calling out greetings to one another as they went, some gathering together briefly in groups, talking and laughing before dispersing and then re-grouping with others, the background sound of people and chatting gradually intensifying throughout the afternoon. Karen and Bob were obviously quite well known and were cheerily greeted by many of the others as they arrived or passed by, some stopping for a quick chat on their way through. It started to dawn on me that most of the people here knew one another to a greater or lesser degree and had obviously been attending these jamborees on an ongoing basis for some time. A secret little micro-world where they could comfortably be and do whatever they wanted without offending anyone or being judged.

While we sat there, watching as the group continued to build in number, Bob and Karen talked me through the format and protocols involved with group swinging in this kind of set up. Over the next few hours there would be general mingling and a chance to get acquainted with people as well as to assess who might be available for what. This would continue while people cooked and ate in their various groups. After that, people would head off to wherever drew them. Essentially, once games had started, the rule was that if a light was on in a caravan and the curtains were not drawn, that was effectively an invitation to voyeurs to watch whatever was going on inside through the window. If the door had also been left open, that was an invitation to enter for a better view or, possibly, but not necessarily, to participate. It all sounded simple enough.

At around seven o'clock people began to gather around the central area, some to light their barbecues, campfires or whatever while others were just drinking and drifting among the various groups. Again, it was obvious that a lot of these people knew one another well and I discovered that these were indeed regular events, taking place several times a year all around the country, sometimes even abroad, and that people did tend to return regularly and become part of the extended group. This part of the evening was apparently the time when arrangements for the evening could be made once everyone had got a feel for who would be where, and offering what, later on in the evening. I set off into the throng and introduced myself to a few people. The atmosphere was friendly; everyone seemed very open, inclusive and willing to accommodate a newcomer so I got a lot of information and suggestions about what was planned and what I might like to get involved with.

Some of the campers were attractive, some less so, but, if I'm to be completely honest, on the whole, many of them were of fairly limited appeal. There were a few women in the crowd who caught my eye, though, and I felt sure I would be able find enough entertainment for myself from the choice available. One woman, in particular, seemed nice a slim brunette, probably in her late thirties, who I'd seen emerging from a motorhome pitched about four spaces away from my caravan and who had been, with her husband, one of the people who had stopped to chat to Karen and Bob while we were sitting together. I only spoke to her briefly but when I mentioned that I would be hanging out with Bob and Karen, her reaction made me think I might see her there too and I hoped I might be able to grab some time with her later. I did speak to the lady who was the only other person there who was not part of a couple. She had arrived with one of the older couples, and I found that she was actually in an ongoing arrangement with them but was engaging more with the wife, having sex with her while the husband would watch. They were, as I was mostly finding, open to increasing the size of their party and asked if I would like to join them but I had to decline, I'm afraid that one really didn't appeal. As people finished eating, they were all gradually congregating around a large open fire-pit, eventually forming one extended group as the last stragglers joined, the laughter and chatter building up all the while until it reached quite an exuberant level.

As well as talking to people who were keen to broadcast the fact that they had a makeshift glory-hole set up, which all the men present were welcome to come and make use of, several people had casually mentioned that some kind of group sex session, or orgy, was being organised too. The glory-hole thing doesn't really appeal to me, as I've mentioned before, but the concept of an orgy made me prick up my ears, being something I'd never had the opportunity to experience before. In all honesty, it wasn't something that had even crossed my mind up to this point and I wasn't entirely sure if I was up for it or not, but I certainly wanted to find out more. Once I'd circumnavigated my way back to Karen and Bob, I asked them what they knew about it, wanting to find out whether it was something that was on offer every time and if they'd ever got involved with one themselves. According to them, there was generally a lot of talk about it at these gatherings but, if it actually ended up happening at all, there generally wasn't a huge turnout with, at best, generally fewer than ten people getting involved. It didn't sound quite so Bacchanalian put like that and I felt my interest in this particular one waning, although the general thought did log itself somewhere in the memory bank to be possibly explored later. Word had obviously got around about me being single as I was being inundated with offers, however, Bob told me that he and Karen had arranged a surprise for me anyway so I happily submitted to that as a start point, deciding to let the rest of the night unfold as it would. Gradually, everyone had started drifting away so we headed off back to Karen and Bob's caravan.

Once there, we all casually and with great merriment, got naked and poured ourselves more drinks. Bob and Karen were giggling, smirking and generally looking a bit furtive which got my radar up a little as I had no idea what the surprise they had in store for me might be. Not that I was overly worried but they obviously found the plan quite an entertaining one. Eventually, I was told to go lie on the bed, which I did, slightly amused, laying there obediently as Karen tied a blindfold over my eyes. Instantly, I was listening out for clues and thought I heard the caravan door close quietly but couldn't be sure. So I just lay there listening and waiting for a minute or so, hearing the odd whisper and some quiet shuffling in the background but nothing more until the sensation of breath on the top of my leg, then a tongue tracing its way up my cock to the tip and circling before tracing back down again. Hands (with a mercifully feminine-seeming touch) came into play, more tongue tracing and then lips finally taking me in. I was pretty sure this wasn't Karen, a different style altogether, but it was very feminine, very enjoyable and I was totally happy to recline there and let it all happen.

I could hear Karen and Bob's voices faintly in the background as they talked in the kitchen. 'Well, whoever you are, I know you're not Karen' I said, addressing the owner of the lips which were now gliding rhythmically up and down my shaft. There was no response from the lips, but Karen had obviously heard me and came through to make some jokey comment or other. Whoever it was attached to my cock was doing a pretty good job though and it was becoming more difficult to focus on anything other than the fact that I was starting to tingle and in danger of letting fly. I made a comment to that effect and was slightly relieved when the pace slowed. Wouldn't want to use up my ammunition reserves too early on this mission. Shortly afterwards, I felt hands behind my head untying the blindfold which was slowly taken away.

Moment of truth.

Thankfully, the sight that greeted me was the pretty brunette I'd spotted earlier, kneeling by the bed, her hand still teasingly stroking me. I confess I did quietly heave a sigh of relief as there were certainly a few women at this gathering I'd have been less pleased to see in that position not to mention that, although I'd become convinced early on it was a woman at work, I wouldn't have put it past them to assign a bloke to the job just for a laugh either. 'David', said Karen, firing a cheeky wink in my direction, 'meet my sister, Denise.' 'Well, how very nice to meet you again' I said, giving her a relieved grin, while in my mind the concept of more 'fun with sisters' presented itself as a rather pleasing idea. Denise's husband had been watching her performance too and now proceeded to join in, as did Bob and Karen, the five of us spending the next hour or two mixing and matching between us all in a mini orgy of our own. Great fun but a bit cramped to be honest in that little caravan bedroom. I know it was always going to be pretty intimate but there were just too many arms and legs to fit into such a small space.

At around midnight, I extricated myself, satisfied but exhausted. I wandered off towards my caravan happy to get some air and suddenly a little intrigued to see what else might be happening around the site. Things were still sounding pretty rowdy all around and I couldn't resist investigating, taking a quick look through a few of the 'invitation' windows on my way past. I guess there were around fifteen campers and caravans with lights on inside and curtains open, four or five of them with their doors open too. There was much the same scenario going on in most of the dens I glanced into as there had been at Bob and Karen's, but with a bit of variation on the theme. Some hand-tying and mild S&M in one, a solo couple in another, a drunken group in one of the doors-open vans who seemed to be trying to find as many ways to imbibe alcohol from one another's orifices and appendages as possible and appeared to be having an absolute riot doing so. I watched, mildly fascinated, as a rounded gent just in

237

front of the window was busy compressing the breasts of the woman standing in front of him with his hands. The woman was holding a bottle of Absolut from which she poured a generous shot into the makeshift cup he had created between her breasts. They then attempted to transfer this to his mouth by using her ample cleavage as a vodka-luge, his messy and only semi-successful efforts noisily cheered on by several others before one of them stepped forward to take a turn. It looked quite a fun game and I was almost tempted to pop my head in through the door until I saw another couple, woman on her back with her legs wedged up against her shoulders while her partner poured his drink into her...cup...and messily attempted to retrieve the contents. That game also looked quite amusing until I realised that 'he' was, in fact, a she, and not a particularly pretty one at that. Like most guys, I'm, in theory, all for a bit of girl-on-girl action but I have to admit the unexpected sight of that was a bit off-putting. It wasn't like it is in the movies and I had, of course, been spoilt a bit by the visual Eden of Leigh and Jenna. I watched one more attempt at the cleavage vodka-luge and moved on. There was no sign of the mooted gangbang, which was mildly disappointing as I'd have liked the chance to get some kind of handle on what the set up was for one of those.

My late-night wander had been quite entertaining but although my mind could have spent longer watching, might even have tried persuading me to join in with one or two, my body was starting to object strongly. I was absolutely knackered, way beyond getting involved with anything more, what with all the drinking and shagging that had already gone on that night, so I took in one quick final circuit and headed off to bed.

I woke the next morning to sounds of laughter and people calling to one another faintly permeating the walls of my already oven-hot caravan. Feeling dazed and jaded I eventually stumbled outside at around ten o'clock, more to escape the stifling heat inside than any great desire to be getting up. Wandering over to where quite a few people people were gathering in the central area to cook and eat breakfast, it seemed that everyone who was up and about seemed in extremely high spirits, though the depleted numbers compared to the previous evening were no surprise since I refused to believe that hangovers hadn't claimed at least a few of the late-night revellers. It was almost a party atmosphere again.and I tuned in to a few conversations between people who were animatedly sharing anecdotes about the previous night's activities. I heard some discussion about the gang-bang, which apparently had actually gone ahead and seemed to have been thoroughly enjoyed by those who'd got involved. Hearing a few of the stories I was half thinking that I might give it a go if I found myself back in this party of happy swinging campers again. There were a few I might have sidestepped but I'm sure I could have found enough fun to keep me going and there's something about the thought of all those bodies together that I find quite enticing.

Sadly, however, that was the last time I saw Karen and Bob. We parted on good terms and I did send them a couple of messages over the following weeks but didn't hear back. I don't know why, perhaps they just wanted to keep things fresh and had moved on, who knows, but I was grateful to them for introducing me to the Caravan Swingers experience. It's certainly one that stands out in the memory and an insight into something new, which I might never have experienced otherwise.

Reflecting back on that weekend I realised that it was really a physical manifestation of what actually occurs on the websites, just with all the potential prospects on-site. The equivalent of profile scanning was the arrival and set-up time where everyone was watching to see who was available to potentially interact with. The subsequent gathering, eating and socialising while discussing possibilities for future play was the 'preliminary meet' bit. Essentially the same system is operated just with progress on a more immediate timescale and done in person rather than from behind a computer screen. A bit like speed dating but with instant sex potential. Twenty-four hours of swinging saturation, which I had thoroughly enjoyed every minute of.

I was starting to wonder, however, if I was getting just a little bit addicted to this whole thing. I'd seen and done so much by now that new experiences, even group ones like this weekend, had taken on an air of almost normality. Would it ever be possible to take it all back to a standard, 'monogamous relationship' level and be completely happy there? Was that something I even wanted any more? I had known as I was working my way through all these different scenarios that they would change me, or at least change my perceptions a bit. The problem with that is that you can't un-learn things. Life doesn't allow you the choice to move backwards in time. All our decisions and actions take their effect and have their eventual impact on our personal evolution. I had given this notion at least a little thought back in the early days and had gone ahead anyway so there was not much virtue in agonising about it now. Rather too late for that. Whatever the eventual consequences, I'd chosen my path and now I must walk it.

Baby, Don't Worry

The fact that I was on this mission for my own therapy perhaps made me more than averagely conscious of what others might be wanting or needing out of it too and it always gave me the greatest pleasure to feel that I'd had a mutually therapeutic experience with someone and helped them on their own journey in some way. I'd been approached by a couple from the Brighton area, Kay and John, who had been married for many years but were struggling with sex because John had developed a psychological problem which had killed his sex drive entirely. He had sought help from various sources but nothing had improved his predicament and over the course of a few emails, some written by Kay but most written by John, I learned that they had last had any kind of sexual interaction eight years previously. Understandably, Kay had found John's withdrawal from that side of their relationship difficult on both a personal and physical level and this situation seemed to be in danger of breaking up the marriage although that didn't appear to be what either of them wanted to happen.

We organised a first meet at a coffee shop tucked below the imposing castle which perches above the medieval market town of Arundel. I arrived to find them already there and sitting at a table. It was fairly busy in the cafe but they were easy enough to spot since not only had we shared pictures but their anxious looking faces would have given them away to me regardless. Despite this, the meet went extremely well. The background clatter and chatter masked the sound of our voices, making them feel less conspicuous as we talked generally about all sorts of things until they both started to seem more comfortable, their ease growing visibly as the minutes ticked by until we had settled into a much more natural flow and, in fact, found that we got on pretty well. Slowly, the conversation moved on to potential progress, which rolled on into an arrangement to meet at mine the following weekend.

In hindsight, the coffee shop hadn't been a particularly good place to meet as it had proved difficult to really open up the conversation with other people at tables so close by, so there were quite a few messages exchanged afterwards about the setup and how things might pan out. These flitted back and forth over the week, many expressing John's anxiety about the whole arrangement and some jitters from Kay too as it had been so long since she'd had sex at all she was worried it might not go too well. I reassured her that I would be as gentle as she needed me to be and that she would be setting the pace for this one. I also made it very clear that if she wanted to bail at any point then that would be absolutely fine, we would just call a halt there and then. There were no obligations on either side to go through with it, especially as she had been so honest and upfront about the circumstances. That seemed to settle her mind a great deal but she was still worried that John might change his mind.

Despite their concerns, though, they duly arrived at my door on the following Saturday evening, their nerves apparent once again as I welcomed them in. I had anticipated this and had made sure there was an open bottle of wine and some glasses at the ready. These I placed into their fidgety hands as rapidly as possible, barely managing to suppress a grin as Kay lifted hers to her mouth straightaway and took an enormous glug. I chit-chatted away as I ushered them into the sitting room with their wine and got them comfortably settled on the sofa. Gradually their tension eased, although I didn't get much interaction from John beyond the current state of the traffic and weather. I think he was just trying to switch himself off from the situation really. He didn't seem agitated or there under duress, but I imagine he was struggling to deal with the fact that this was where his condition had led and he gave me the impression that he just wanted it to be over and behind him.

Suddenly, Kay got to her feet and said 'Dave, let's just go and do this before I bottle out'.

Happy to oblige, I stood and turned to John.

'Are you coming up too?' I asked.

'I'd prefer to stay here and watch TV If that's ok?' he replied, quietly.

'Of course, no problem', I said, 'but feel free to pop up any time you want' and, with that, led Kay away and showed her upstairs.

She'd obviously made an effort for the occasion and, looked very nice in a dress which crossed over her front and tied at the waist, showing off a pretty decent figure too, nice, curvy lines if not exactly buxom. She started unzipping her dress, looking a little shy so I turned my attention away while I took off my shirt and jeans. When I looked up she was standing in her underwear, looking a little bashful and sweetly attractive. As I looked at her in appreciation, she started self-consciously covering herself up with her hands, eyes cast down to the floor. I took her by the shoulders and made her look me in the eye.

'You are stunning', I told her, 'You have a beautiful body and you should definitely not be shy of showing it off, you look wonderful'.

David B

She looked like she might cry for a moment so I kissed her very gently by way of distraction and as I felt her start to relax into my arms, lifted her up and laid her on the bed.

'I'm going to be very gentle', I said, 'so don't you worry about anything. Just do whatever you want to do and if you want to stop at any time, you just say the word. Okay?'

She nodded, still looking a bit hesitant, so I ran my hands soothingly over her body while she lay there, still in her underwear, slowly, gradually working towards her more sensitive areas, retreating, then approaching again, ever closer. Soon her face was looking much more relaxed and she was emitting quiet moans as she dropped into her zone. A little longer and she was gently starting to arch and push against my hand. I slid it slowly down under her panties and she shuddered and let out a little cry as I made contact with her clit. I withdrew my hand a little and worked gently around the area for a little longer before allowing it to return. No jumping from her this time, in fact she seemed very responsive now, so I let my hand roam further, fingers gently stroking back and forth, feeling the veritable river of her wetness breaking through. By now she was starting to groan and move about a bit and as I pulled down her bra with my free hand and encased her nipple with my lips she let out a yelp and, with a violent shudder, came hard all over my hand.

'Blimey', I thought, 'it really has been a while for you, girl, hasn't it?' I was fervently hoping that one tiny orgasm wasn't going to be enough for her and that she wasn't about to call time. Luckily, it turned out quite to the contrary. I lay beside her quietly stroking her tummy until her breathing fully slowed again. She still had her eyes closed and I wasn't sure how, or even if, to proceed from here, but her body seemed relaxed so I decided to keep going and see how she responded. I started letting my hand drift further afield now, still keeping what I hoped was a soothing and reassuring feel to it but slowly easing towards the edge of her pretty underwear, then further, drawing the edge a little further down with each stroking movement, trying to read whether this was what she wanted. She was laying perfectly still while this was going on, almost like she was listening, perhaps, but I could sense no anxiety or resistance so I continued onwards until her underwear had been fully removed.

Quietly, I shifted myself over and positioned myself lightly on top of her. Still not sure how gentle she was going to need me to be, I teased her for a moment, making sure everything was nice and wet before slowly starting to ease in. I felt her tense and briefly thought she was going to come again but after half a beat she'd reached down, grabbed me by the buttocks and was hauling me inside like her life depended on it. Guided by her, I just went with the flow and was soon hammering away so hard I thought I might break her. She seemed in a whole other place, eyes closed, moaning and writhing as she clung to me like a limpet. When I paused for a moment she half opened her eyes and I smiled at her. 'Alright?' I asked. I got no more than an unintelligible moan and an arch of her body as a response. I took that as a 'yes' and piled in once more. A few minutes later though, still at full throttle, Kay surprised me by pushing me away. I stopped immediately, worried I might have hurt her or misread her, but was relieved to find that she simply wanted to turn over, twisting herself quickly around before getting to her knees and sitting straight back on me. I hadn't really expected that but it wasn't an unwelcome development and we'd soon resumed our rhythm with her gradually moving forward onto all fours and eventually laying flat out with me on top of her, grinding her into the bed. After a while I could feel the intensity hit a peak and when she indicated that she wanted to turn back over I knew it wouldn't be for long. Sure enough, within what seemed like a few strokes her legs were stiffening and she was off, shuddering her way to oblivion and I was free to let go myself.

We lay there, panting, for a little while. Both of us were, I think, slightly taken aback by the ferocity of what had just occurred. After a while, regular breathing restored, she turned to me.

'I knew I was feeling frustrated but I didn't realise how much I'd really missed sex'. 'Well', I replied, 'you know where I am any time you feel the need again'.

Given my own history, I had an immediate sympathy with how she was feeling.

She gave me a brief hug as we lay there side by side, however, she was immediately concerned about how John was doing on his own downstairs and wanted to go down and see him. She dressed quickly and disappeared off downstairs while I tidied up a bit and followed her a few minutes later, only to find John fast asleep on the sofa with Match of the Day on the telly. We both smiled, her affectionately at John and I with relief that it had all gone so well and I didn't have a squeamish, jittery or possibly angry and frustrated husband to deal with. We sat down and picked up our wine glasses, talking normally over John's sleeping form until he came to with a jump, looking from Kay to me and back before picking up his own wine glass again.

'Everything went OK then?' he asked and we nodded casually. He seemed like a really nice guy.

They left shortly afterwards and I had a text from Kay later letting me know that they were home and all was well. She thanked me for the evening and said she was looking forward to an opportunity for us all to get together again soon. That sounded very promising and I was feeling very pleased with the way it had all gone. Actually, I was hoping I had found what might turn out to be an on-going, regular arrangement. It seemed to stack up perfectly in principle but although I had several more texts from Kay over the following weeks and it all looked good, the messages dried up. I never found out why. I did send a couple more texts but when I had no response I left them alone. If they'd wanted to pursue things further then they would have kept in touch and, whatever the reason, if they'd decided against it then that was, of course, an entirely acceptable choice for them to make. So I left them to it, hoping that things had worked out for them one way or another and quietly acknowledging a sense of fondness for them both after what had actually been, on many levels, quite an emotionally engaging encounter.

David B

White Wedding

As autumn began to loom on the horizon, a text came, out of the blue, asking how I was, what I was up to and was I still on the scene? It took a moment to register who it was from but I was really pleased when I realised it had been sent by Don and Janice, the couple I'd spent such a happy evening with nearly a year previously and who had taken a break from swinging whilst they planned their wedding. I rather assumed that receiving a message from them meant that things had all gone to plan, so I got straight back to them asking how they'd been and how the wedding had gone and also saying how nice it would be to catch up.

It seemed that the wedding had been a great success and they were incredibly happy but that now they were back home they wanted to have a special meet before the wedding euphoria wore off and would I object to getting together for another play date but this time with Janice wearing her wedding dress. I must admit, that request caught me off guard and made me hesitate for just a moment. I felt quite privileged to be asked, as I guessed it would be a special play for them, it was just the prospect of the wedding dress that had momentarily broken my stride. It was still a fairly big, symbolic item for me, having buried my lovely Lynn in hers. However, recalling how much I had enjoyed my time with Don and Janice, I felt inclined to go ahead and got back to them to arrange a rendezvous. We agreed to meet up the following Saturday night, which gave me a few days to ponder this new turn of events and adjust to the idea. I was really looking forward to seeing them again but that rogue memory of the poignant last time I'd seen a woman in a wedding dress did pop to the forefront of my mind more than once.

It wasn't overwhelming me but I was, nonetheless, quietly aware of it.

Saturday dawned bright and breezy. I spent the morning shopping and preparing and the afternoon getting on with some gardening and general tidying up. As the meet time approached I felt a little tinge of tension and it occurred to me then that this rarely, if ever, happened to me these days. I had a hot, relaxing shower, got dressed, lit the fire and then poured myself a soothing glass of wine. Most often, I don't tend to start drinking before my guests arrive but I made an exception this time and was feeling more relaxed by the time they appeared. Janice had the dress in a suit carrier so I wasn't presented with her in full flouncy, white regalia on my doorstep, a fact which relieved me greatly. We greeted each other like long lost friends, ending up having an affectionate group hug in the hall while I congratulated them on their newly acquired marital status, before working our way through towards the fireplace where I dispensed more wine into waiting glasses, including my own, now empty one. To be honest, the moment I saw them all my trepidation was forgotten and I sat comfortably catching up with them both for a while before Janice went off to change into her dress.

Soon, we heard her voice calling from the top of the stairs.

'Are you ready for me boys?'

We responded enthusiastically and made a great deal of appreciative fuss and celebratory noise as she made her way down the stairs. I have to say, she looked sensational. Radiant and still tanned from her honeymoon I wasn't surprised when Don got out his camera and started taking photos. It was a theme which continued throughout the evening as they obviously wanted as many pictures of the *Wedding Dress Adventure* as they could get. It certainly made for an entertaining night as there turned to be no end of artistic and creative things you can do with a camera and a woman in a wedding dress. Some of my favourites were shots we took of her bending over by the fireplace, hands on the mantelpiece and legs spread with her dress hitched up over her bum and a series of 'treats' for her in that position involving tongues, cocks and dildoes. She was enjoying every minute, often playing comically to the camera and making us all roar with laughter as well as producing some very hot mementos for them to enjoy later. They did send a few through to me too and it brings a smile to my face remembering that night. We experimented with lots of location ideas; on the sofa, on the floor, on the stairs and some very tongue in cheek (and tongues in lots of other places) shots in the kitchen of Janice 'cooking', 'blending' and 'washing up' in various compromising positions. I have a shot of her laid back on the worktop with her dress up round her waist and her boobs exposed while I have my face buried between her legs. It is my absolute favourite.

Though we were really enjoying getting creative with the camera show, we were also taking time out in the various locations to indulge ourselves physically too before moving on to the next. By the time we had finished in the kitchen I think we were all at our limits and ended up in a writhing heap on the floor next to the fireplace where we finished things off fairly rapidly, barely needing any encouragement to tip any of us over the brink after all that extended foreplay.

Afterwards, as we sat in the glow from the fire looking through some of the shots we'd taken, it occurred to me that this particular scenario felt as though it represented an important point in my journey. Perhaps more akin to reaching Everest Base Camp rather than claiming to have fully scaled the mountain peak, but proof of progress nonetheless. The fact that I could sit, perfectly contentedly, in the presence of an incredibly happy, newly married couple, with that symbolic wedding dress on full display, and yet feel so comfortable made me realise how far I had come in the past eighteen months in contrast to the previous five or so years between Lynn's death and the start of this more recent chapter. Yes, of course I still loved Lynn and cherished every memory of her but this was the moment I consciously realised I'd finally accepted her passing. Though emphatically never to be forgotten, I had at last laid the ghost of her to rest in my own mind. It had been a gradual process which, unnoticed by me, had been easing by degrees for some time. No doubt there had been other contributory factors such as the support of friends and family, time passing, etc, but looking back over the whole six year period it seemed clear to me that it was my interaction with this liberatingly unorthodox scene which had helped me the most to let go, allowed me to ascend above the clouds of grief and give myself permission to live freely once again.

* * * * *

David B

Time Of My Life

Although I was party to numerous additional encounters during the time period covered here, it was never my intention to write a definitive list. I hope the ones I've chosen to share will have entertained and possibly enlightened you as well as given some idea of the range of potential adult fun experiences lurking out there in the shadows. I have loved reliving each one in the telling but this does seem to be an appropriate point at which to end this book. As with everything in life, doors open and close at different times and the journey moves on. What is written here represents a chapter in my life which I felt I needed to embrace at the time and which has had a profound and, I believe, a positive impact on my life on many levels. The fact that I have chosen to stop adding to the content of this book at this point does not necessarily mean that I intend to stop interacting with websites and potential partners in the future. My encounter rate has, perhaps, reduced a little recently but at this point in time I am still actively adding to my list of experiences whenever the mood takes me.

I have asked myself several questions over the course of living and subsequently writing about these experiences, one being: 'If Lynn were still alive, might we have been tempted to try swinging together at any point?' The answer, I think, is 'probably not', as my memory is of a contented togetherness which I can't imagine having wanted to expand in that way, but who knows what the future would have held and what avenues life might have led us down given more time.

I've also often wondered what Lynn would say to me, if she could, about her views on where life has taken me over the years since she died. Obviously, that's something I'll never know for certain but I suspect that, in the absence of being able to do anything practical to help me herself, she would have condoned and supported any action I undertook to help my own recovery. She had a tremendous sense of fun and adventure and I quite like to think of her watching over me, hooting with laughter at some of the situations I've found myself in from time to time.

Another thing I've asked myself more recently is: 'after all these experiences, could I be, and remain, faithful if I was now to meet another woman and embark on a regular, monogamous relationship?' I believe the answer to that would be a definite 'yes' because although my attitude to sexual interaction has been opened up by exposure to all these different situations, I don't think it represents an essential part of my existence. It has been an eye-opening and liberating episode, which may well have more to offer yet, but I don't think it is something it would be impossible to leave behind. Perhaps I am kidding myself! Perhaps, one day, I will be in a situation where I will find out for certain.

Another question, which a few of those who know what this book contains have asked, is: 'Would I be comfortable telling any future prospective partners about my experiences with swinging?' Again, 'yes', without hesitation. Secrets generally destroy a relationship anyway and lies have a habit of making themselves known sooner or later. Definitely something to be avoided at all costs. Besides, I don't feel the need to conceal what I've done since it isn't something I feel was in any way wrong to do. There was nothing illegal involved although there may be those who will condemn my actions for one reason or another.

The most important question of all for me, though, is 'Have I benefited from these experiences and what have they helped me to achieve?' The answer to this is just what I hoped it would be at the start of this venture and the reason I landed on this path in the first place. It seems to me that aside from dealing with my physical frustration, all of these encounters have somehow helped me lay to rest a lot of the trauma and issues of the past and have given me a forum in which I've had space to process the emotional minefield in my own time without that depression-enhancing feeling that life was simply passing me by. I'm not a psychologist and I'm not entirely sure quite why or how this has happened but the proof for me is in comparing how I feel now with how I felt, and behaved, before this began.

For the years prior to finding this solution I would suffer intense mood swings, sometimes resulting in deep bouts of depression, which would often lead to me drinking to excess in binge sessions that would lay waste to me for days. I would also withdraw socially for long periods of time, burying the black pain that descended on me by retreating into abject solitude, abandoning my friends and dropping all communication with people until I somehow clawed my way, alone, back to the surface at some later date. This is no longer the case, in fact, aside from the immediate aftermath of losing Milton, I have not suffered with depression in almost two years. I feel much more in control and no longer feel the need to try to protect myself from the triggers which would once have sent me plummeting into the gloom. I doubt the emotional journey is yet complete, despite the distance run thus far, but I suspect that any remaining hurdles will present themselves only if I embark at some point on a romantic relationship. Although that opportunity has not, as yet, presented itself I'm no longer averse to the idea, in fact I have no negative feelings towards the concept at all.

So, as things stand at present, with the closing of this book, I doubt that it will mean the end of my swinging career. I have thoroughly enjoyed exploring this most interesting and entertaining of worlds and until such time as my circumstances change and require me to do so, I don't feel particularly inclined to give it up. In one sense, the result I needed has been achieved, and in that respect I'd be happy to hang up my prowler's hat and call it a job well done. However, I embraced this lifestyle quite wholeheartedly, after my initial struggles with it, and I have a suspicion that it will continue to be something which holds a significant level of appeal.

Perhaps I'm not quite ready to leave this all behind just yet.

* * * * *

David B

Post Script

I first met Dave a year or so after he lost Lynn, so I never got to meet her and I'm sad about that. He was one of those people with whom I felt an instant connection and we soon became good friends, seeing each other socially on a regular basis within a group of mutual friends.

Although I missed the early days of his bereavement, it was painfully obvious how raw he still felt about his situation when we first discussed it and I was aware that he would take himself off and seal himself away, sometimes for weeks on end, when things got too much. He knew that we, as a group of friends, were perfectly happy to tolerate a bit of misery and that he was welcome to bring that misery out and share the burden with us, but he chose to retreat and regroup rather than spread the pain around. None of us having had much experience of bereavement on this level, we would message our concerns, assure him of our support and then, sometimes reluctantly, respect his need for privacy and step back. I think we all felt a bit helpless, as anyone dealing with a fellow, grief-stricken soul probably does at times. Sadly, of course, there is no magic wand to make everything better and watching someone you care for suffer is an awful experience.

Gradually we noticed an improvement though. Longer 'up times', shorter and fewer 'down times' and more regular glimpses of the cheeky, good-natured and upbeat man at the heart of Dave. It was good to see.

When he eventually confided in a couple of us about the secret method he had employed to help combat his demons, my immediate reaction was a mixture of amazement and excitement. Dave's not the sort of chap you would look at and immediately label 'Swinger' by any means and it was no great surprise to me to discover, when I started working with him on this book, that he'd been something of an accidental tourist finding adventures in a foreign land, rather than a predatory sex fiend.

I am so glad that he has chosen to share his experiences in this way and especially pleased to be the one who got to assist him in getting this written work off the ground. It has been the most interesting project I could have wished to be involved with. I do recall messaging him about two days into the start of the writing saying 'Please, Dave, tell me this is all true. Please promise me you didn't make this up!' Of course, I already knew the answer and anyone who has met Dave will understand that sentiment, as he is, quite simply, one of the most genuine people you could wish to meet, but some of the situations in his notes just amazed me to the point of having to ask.

What overwhelmingly stands out to me, as a friend of Dave's who has watched him pick his way through the emotional warzone of the past few years, is the undeniable change in his sense of general inner contentment. After seeing him for so long operating at such a low ebb it has been a joy and a relief to see how he has returned to the consistent-natured, affable and happy person he plainly always was at heart, his core self now restored.

Although I'm sure the anguish of Lynn's death will always remain in his memory, it surfaces rarely these days and he is fully engaged with the here and now, lively and amusing and relentlessly keen to get involved with or organise social events and see friends, although he is also perfectly happy in his own company, grounded and secure enough to enjoy

257

David B

whatever situation he happens to find himself in. It seems clear to me that this exercise has kick-started his life again.

Swinging is not something I had the first idea about before starting work on this collaboration but my eyes have been opened and I've learned a thing or two! It's perhaps not something I feel the inclination to try for myself but I have greatly enjoyed this little window on an unfamiliar world and hope that anyone reading his story will feel the same.

Thank you for including me in this most entertaining of ventures, Dave, it has been a real pleasure.

Zara

* * * * *

Printed by Amazon Italia Logistica S.r.l.
Torrazza Piemonte (TO), Italy